PRAISES FOR RAISING THE BAR
AS A HIGH SCHOOL STUDENT

'Raising The Bar As A High School Student' brings a fresh perspective to how we view young people and the issues they face. – **Samuel Idem**

In the words of the author, "your situation should never define you" and "the height of your potential depends solely on you. " This book is all you need to lead you through the path to raising the bar as a high school student. – **Emem Sylvia Essien, Entrepreneur**

As much as some people have tried to deny it, there are specific keys to success in both academics and life, and this book has boldly revealed, to young adults, what those keys are. – **Dele Aina, Author of Chalk Power**

The rich points developed in 'Raising the Bar as a High School Student' are valuable guides to bring anyone to the zenith of achievements in life. – **Olubanke Ohunenese, Vice-Principal of Chrisland High School Ikeja**

A must-read primer for anyone considering high school. Read this book, and learn from one of the best. – **Victoria Onwuasor, Author & Lawyer**

A terrific, engaging, and much-needed book that will equip teens with powerful tools to raise the bar and reach their full potential. – **Sylvester Jenkins III, Author of From Combat to Comeback**

A nicely-spun book. More grease to your elbow, Charles. – **Tunbosun Aiyedehin, Nollywood Actress**

A success story told through a collection of personal experiences, serving as a manual for those wishing to advance in their studies, careers, and even relationships. — **Tonia Okojie, Nollywood Actress, Teen Mentor, and Entrepreneur**

The book simplifies for high school students what adults are still trying to figure out. Therefore, consider this book a safe haven because I was blessed by it. — **Toluwalase Awoderu, Founder of Lantern Lessons International.**

This book recalibrates the mindset of its reader making them uncomfortable with being average. — **Efuna Emmanuel, Founder of CareerHeft Africa**

The book would empower the young generation on the path of excellence and help them make the right choices. — **Odunayo Akinboboye, Kids coach**

RAISING THE BAR

AS A HIGH SCHOOL STUDENT

Editing & Cover design by Andrewdaniels Creatives, Lagos, Nigeria.

Phone no: +234 802 292 2964

Website: www.andrewdan.com

ISBN: 979-8-218-03726-0

Charles Obirinanwa Group.

DEDICATION

My mother, whose unending love for me enables me to overcome obstacles.
My family and friends, whose constant encouragement keeps me going.
Every high school student who applies the lessons in this book, and raises the
bar in all aspects of life.

TABLE OF CONTENTS

o · · · · · · · · · o

FOREWORD

○ · · · · · · · · ○

Every time I turned a page in this book, I was giddy with anticipation, wondering what lessons and wisdom would be revealed to me on the next page. That is to say, this book not only grabs but holds your attention.

In Raising the Bar as a High School Student, Charles provides concrete tips that young adults can use to improve their lives. As a successful young man who is making a difference, readers can rest assured that Charles' words offer a clear path to success and happiness.

As a parent and teacher, I find this work to be very inspiring, insightful, and TIMELY. I think it is especially important now that our young generation is often distracted by things like social media and other unwholesome attention grabbers.

Charles has boldly attempted in this book to show high school students the sure path to success and excellence, not only in academics but also in life. I am confident that anyone who follows the advice in this book will excel far beyond high school. Raising the Bar as a High School Student is a must-read for students and parents. I'm sure you'll find it as inspiring as I did.

Dele Aina,
Award-winning author and CEO of J2 Consulting.

INTRODUCTION

Leadership, human capacity building, societal literacy, and other topics are among the foundations on which many great books are built today. Yet, very few are focused on the grassroots; that age-old foe that we must all overcome in order to enter "the real world" and formally ascend onto the platform of "freedom," "leadership," or "adulthood."

Although it would appear that nothing short of superhuman abilities is required to succeed in high school, this was not the case for all of us; at least, it was not the case for me. I had no telepathy to rely on during tests, nor super speed, during sports.

Hence, this guide—A gift from me to you, and others, like us, without superpowers, who only wish to graduate from high school in style.

This is an enchiridion of experiences and tips centered on your growth and evolution, as a student and an individual.

The number of high school students in the world has exploded beyond counting, with students now accounting for a significant portion of any country's youth population. In fact, one could say that seven in every ten young people are students (and of those, half are high school students). As a result, high school students account for a significant portion of any country's population.

Physically, emotionally, mentally, or psychologically, students go through a lot. The consequences of these problems are usually visible in their level of productivity. The average student would struggle with issues such as poor grades, and high expectations from parents, teachers, friends, and even acquaintances. Have you ever met a complete stranger who thinks you're the

1

next Einstein just because you wear glasses? That acquaintance has now placed the responsibility of living up to society's expectations of glasses wearers on you.

What about peer pressure, looks, habits, dating, and so on? These issues and many more can become huge burdens on students, especially when handled poorly by students, their families, and society. The world around us may often brush aside these issues, under the notion that they are 'trivial', whereas, they are not. Most societies are not built in a way that accommodates the evolving teenager, which is quite unfortunate. Nonetheless, if you find that this has been a hindering factor to you, note that your situation should never define you. The opinions of society should be your stepping stone and not a brick wall. The height of your potential depends solely on you.

Life is not a bed of roses, and neither is your journey as a high school student. With its many layers comes a great deal of responsibility. You must juggle between classes, extracurriculars, and one that many have struggled to add to the mix, their personal lives.

A friend once told me that life is easy and that all we need to do is follow certain principles and instructions. I believed otherwise, and I tried to convince him that life is tough, but he stood by his statement. Baffled as to why anyone would think that the daily grit and grind I have gone through was a cakewalk, I asked God for insight. That night, as I prayed, I was drawn to Hosea, a book in the Bible.

"My people are destroyed for lack of knowledge: because thou hast rejected knowledge, I will also reject thee, that thou shalt be no priest to me: seeing thou hast forgotten the law of thy God, I will also forget thy children." - **Hosea 4:6**

Knowledge is a powerful tool! It is, in my opinion, simply a set of instructions for living life on 'Easy Difficulty.' No one can achieve their goals in life unless they adhere to certain principles and follow specific instructions. Every aspect of life operates according to certain laws; therefore, if you want to excel in a specific area, you must follow the set instructions, to excel in that area.

Indeed, I dare to say that this is a book for everyone because contrary to popular belief, raising the bar is not limited to academics; rather, it explains an overall improvement in all aspects of one's life.

Every single one of us has the ability to be excellent and to be the best version of ourselves. As Aristotle believed, excellence is "not an act, but a habit". Even so, as I previously stated, when you apply the laws that guide you to success, it will become clearer and more evident. I like to think of ourselves as bank accounts with an initial deposit of excellence; that bar-raising characteristic, if you will. This deposit can only grow if you invest time and effort. As such, we can only fully harness our innate excellence when we choose to be different, and live by principles and set instructions.

A wise man once said; "we walk by common sense, we run by principles, but we fly by instruction". You don't train a child to walk; a child learns to walk by common sense; an athlete, on the other hand, does not win medals by chance; he runs by the track's standards or principles, and a pilot flies a plane by the manuals, instructions, or commands. In your flight to excellence, you will need commands and would need to obey these commands stringently.

Raising the bar as a high school student is basically about seeing yourself excel as a young student in terms of excellence. As a result, I advise that you not only skim through the pages of this book but that you read it intentionally. And, very importantly, put every knowledge acquired from it into action because it instills wisdom— the application of knowledge. From now on, your school experiences will change for the better. I, for one, have never finished a good book and remained unchanged; there has always been a significant shift. Your journey begins right now.

Your bar-raising friend,

Charles.

CHAPTER 1

○ · · · · · · · · ○

A THOUSAND MILES JOURNEY
BEGINS WITH ONE STEP

"Everybody has a different journey. Everybody has a different path, and you don't really know what to expect. All you know is to just keep plugging away, and you hope something will come through and something will happen"
— Grace Gealey

My first day of high school was indeed a life-changing experience for me. Going down memory lane, the events of that day are still fresh in my mind. My brother and my cousin were dropped off at Chrisland High School when the car came to a close. Then, with my siblings, Mom, and aunt, I descended the car as well.

It was shortly after the Ebola epidemic had ended. Indeed, the outbreak effectively put a stop to a wide range of public activities. After we had stayed home for an extra 2 weeks or more, the government issued a directive for academic activities to resume for the new session. Starting high school made me feel ecstatic. I was a step closer to finally going to college.

It was electrifying, but I'll never forget the counsel my 6th-grade teacher offered me: "Remember our 6th-grade class' appellation; remember to be a positive changer who would utilize diligence, commitment, and the fear of God." Those words, I'll admit today, guided me throughout my time in high school.

As human beings, we are only sojourners here on earth — temporary residents, if you will. As Chris Stapleton accurately put it; "I'm just a traveler on this earth"-- We all are. You are, without a doubt, a traveler on a journey in life, and your high school is a mandatory stop that you must make. Arriving at the gate and entering the school grounds only serves to emphasize that you have taken a step further in the journey of life. How you approach this part of your journey determines whether or not you'll reach your desired destination in life.

The truth is that the majority of middle schoolers are unprepared for the realities of high school. I had no idea what to expect, and nor did I think it was that important to be prepared -Yes, I wasn't always the academically astute author writing to you now-. In reality, I saw it as a straightforward path for me to follow. You can't hold it against me. I've always found life seemingly easy. As a matter of fact, I was one of the best students in my class, 90th percentile, even.

I always seemed to land on my feet, every time. As a result, I never went out of my way to prepare for anything because I had the misguided belief that life was easy. Nevertheless, I am grateful that I was oblivious to the challenges I would face in high school. Who knows, maybe if I had, I would not have enrolled in the first place.

*"If all the challenges were understood at the start of a long journey, most of us would never start at all". – **Dan Rather.***

There will always be an assurance!

One reality of life is that many people would opt out of achieving most goals if they had a glimpse of what the road to achieving those goals would be like. Many will give up before the race starts if they are to compete against an athlete with many accolades to his credit. This is why we are frequently shielded from the reality of knowing what the road ahead will be like. It's no surprise that many people will opt-out and forget that true success awaits at the end of any such path.

*"People will insist on building high and wide barriers directly in your path, often with the intent of closing you in. If you treat these obstacles like fencing walls, they will prove mightily so. I choose to see them as grand towers meant to be scaled and conquered, providing an added victory as well as a great view of the journey ahead." - **Richelle E. Goodrich***

The path to anything that makes you successful is never easy. If you want to be at the forefront, you must overcome some obstacles.

If you expect to have a sense of what your entire high school experience will be like, you may find yourself waiting indefinitely. This is not because

5

your imagination is deceptive, but rather because it may lead you to believe that you should end the journey before it begins.

Consider my own experience: my journey through high school initially appeared to be endless and fruitless. What precisely did I do? I appeared to be a sojourner as if this was a phase in my life that would usher me into a new chapter. But it all worked out in the end. Now I'm here, eager to share my discoveries with you while also encouraging you to reflect on them.

"Don't be afraid of your fears. They're not there to scare you. They're there to let you know that something is worth it." - C. JoyBell C.

Throughout my career, I've had to learn that the phrase "fear" only exists in the mind once the thinker has given it a lot of consideration. Fear has no power to conquer a potential because it only exists to demonstrate that action is worthwhile.

"Our greatest fear isn't that we're insufficient. Our deepest fear is that we are incredibly strong. Our light, not our darkness, is what scares us the most. 'Who am I to be brilliant, gorgeous, talented, fabulous?' we wonder. Who are you not to be, after all? You have a lot of promise. Playing tiny isn't good for the world. There's nothing enlightened about shrinking so that others don't feel insecure in your presence. As youngsters, we are all meant to shine. We were born with the ability to realize the potentials that have been placed inside us. It is not only in a few of us; it is in all of us. And by allowing our own light to shine, we automatically allow others to do the same." - Marianne Williamson

Whatever challenges we face as human beings, fear should never impede us from overcoming them. So get over your apprehensions about high school. Many students get cold feet and are nervous on their first day of high school, and some remain that way as sophomores, juniors, and seniors. My experience, on the other hand, was not the same. I talked with my elementary school classmates who had transferred to the same high school as me; I made new friends, and I quickly adjusted. I assure you that there is nothing to be afraid of! You're about to start a new chapter in your life, one that will be filled with growth and prosperity. Then, while you're aware that you'll need to give it your all to make the most of your new adventure, you should keep a positive attitude.

Be prepared!

Preparation is an integral part of building a solid foundation for whatever you plan on accomplishing. This is what it looks like:

You practice, you keep practicing, and will not stop practicing until the instant you reach the moment you have prepared for.

"Give me six hours to chop down a tree and I will spend the first four sharpening the ax. I will prepare and someday my chance will come." -
Abraham Lincoln

These words should motivate you, and you should consider how you may manage your preparation strength since it is important in your High School responsibilities.

So, my question is, are you prepared? If you believe you are, what prepared you?

Many parents take the initiative to sit with their children and discuss how to make the most of their High School years, whereas others leave their children to their own devices. Now, regardless of your position, it is neither an advantage nor a disadvantage for you because you are the only one who can prepare you! Nobody else can get you ready for high school or any other thing, except you.

How do I get prepared?

Many students have often claimed that pep talks from parents, teachers, and guardians are insufficient, while some appreciate them. Of course, this is unsurprising, since every one of us is different. Some people grasp things quickly, while others may need to pay attention to them for a long time before they can stand. Many students have told us about how they transformed into unrecognizable people in high school; shadows of their former selves. Unbeknownst to their parents, the children have grown into completely different individuals than they were before. It does happen!

As a result, it is critical that you decide to prepare yourself, and that whatever your parents, teachers, or anyone else you look up to feed you is complementary. Think of it as adding more sugar to your already sugared donuts.

Here are a few steps that I believe will help you prepare for high school:

- **The Mindset:** It all starts with the mind. Our minds are the most valuable asset we have as humans. Its complexity, as well as its ability to absorb and transform information into knowledge, make it an exceptional tool. Nonetheless, it is a tool, and tools are useless without someone to use them. Because the mind is a tool for you to use, it is subordinate to you. As a result, it should be impossible for it to control you, but you should be able to control it. It will be your greatest ally the moment you begin the hard work required to succeed.

  I have faith in you to do so.

  I have always set a high standard for myself because of the encouragement of so many wonderful people in my life.

  Throughout my high school years, this mindset helped me strive for greatness. I remember telling myself one day that I would graduate as the Head Boy of my high school, and it all came true. Why? Because my mind had envisioned it from the start. I was determined to be the best.

- **Believe it and stick with it:** If you believe and stick to your vision of what you want, you will have everything you need to achieve it. I was convinced in high school that I would be recognized. I believed it and stuck to it from the beginning to the end of my High School years. I never lost sight of that goal. Keep your objectives in mind at all times. Maintain your trust in them and your dedication to them. Take my word for it: there will always be a time when you will be remembered; when you will stand out from the crowd. That day will undoubtedly come.

- **Work towards it:** The temptation to be conceited is the biggest contender to the realization of any dream. Commitment and diligence have never killed anyone; they are simply stepping stones to achieving your goals. In elementary school, we used to sing a rhyme that went like this: "Good, better, best, I'll never rest; until my good is better and my better, best." Those are some powerful lyrics, capable of producing any great success story. It is never too late to begin, and if you have already begun, don't become complacent. What you want out of life is more than a fantasy or a figment of your

8

imagination. Consider it a destination that you have yet to reach. As a result, KEEP MOVING.

- **Seek Knowledge:** Whatever you achieve in life must be a solution to an existing problem. If it does not, the individual is wasting their time. Knowledge is light! It can make any difficult situation easier for you if used correctly.

  This is where encouragement from parents, teachers, and role models can help. If they don't call, please go to them; that's why I said you are the only one who can get you ready. Don't wait for someone to call you for advice; instead, go after them and allow yourself to be impacted. You cannot place a price on experience, it is simply priceless. As such, try to learn from the experiences of others.

  Reading can also help you broaden your horizons. Attending training(s), seminars, and webinars can help you prepare. You can join clubs, organizations, and groups of deserving students who share your goals for success. The main goal is to be endowed with knowledge, which should not be underestimated. However, you must exercise caution when gathering information. Everything you hear or see must be filtered.

- **Be Committed to Something:** The importance of commitment in everything we do cannot be overstated. Because there is always an end and a beginning, there is always a specific place for you as humans. This is the time to become more active and committed to your goals than ever before. You must be firm in your plans because they can only be created by you. Clear your mind of all negative thoughts. "I'm confident I'll do well." It's a simple affirmation that can work wonders. It is the impact of the words, not their length, that is important. Accept more commitment to making these ideas a reality in your life because the plans for you are wonderful. Today, my friend, you're on your way to the summit!

You now have an advantage over others; all you need to do now is ensure that you are committed to whatever the outcome of taking these steps is. You will be better prepared and equipped than ever before.

Confirm your Preparation: Be Confident That You Are Ready

Auto mechanics have a distinct personality. When they finish working on

9

a vehicle, they will start it and test drive it to ensure that any modifications they have made have taken effect. That is the mindset we should have when it comes to high school readiness. Most people will be willing to prepare, but only a small percentage will confirm whether or not they are truly prepared for high school. Never make that mistake.

You must confirm that you are prepared, and if you are not, you must retreat and figure out what you need to do to get ready for this new phase of your life. It is pointless to fool yourself into believing you are prepared for a higher level of anything when you are not. You must correct any potential misconceptions or bad habits now to avoid the consequences later.

You don't want to start school and fall behind. You must confirm your level of preparation and be honest with yourself.

*"Champions do not become champions when they win the event, but in the hours, weeks, months, and years they spend preparing for it. The victorious performance itself is merely the demonstration of their championship character." - **Alan Armstrong***

Alan Armstrong declares that the circumstances surrounding today's great champions are based on the hours, weeks, months, and years they spend architecting for preparation, not the results they achieve; not their accurately known victorious performance, but "the hours, weeks, months, and years they spend architecting for preparation". As a result, how potential dreamers and High School students deal with preparation is the key to their efficiency.

Previous High School students who are now well-known in the world spoke about how serious and meticulous they are with their preparations for anything. As a result, I implore you not to rush to determine whether you are ready. "The race is not for the swift". In fact, life is a journey rather than a race. As a result, patience and intelligence triumph over speed.

Anyone who sits down and consciously plans the next phase of their life in this manner is bound for greatness. It is your natural right to be exceptional, and you have prepared yourself to embark on the journey.

This will be one of the most unforgettable experiences of your life. A few years ago, I was walking past the Chrisland High School gates, in Ikeja, Lagos. I entered regally, certain that I would leave my mark on the school. I believe you are capable of doing the same.

It is the beginning of a new day for you. Be thankful that you have arrived at this point. It's time to get involved in more adventures that will allow you to live the A-class student life you've always wanted. So let us delve deeper!

CHAPTER 2

o · · · · · · · · o

SET THOSE GOALS
NOW!

*"If you want to be happy, set a goal that commands your thoughts,
liberates your energy, and inspires your hopes"*
*— **Andrew Carnegie***

"Goal-setting" is a term you must have heard as a teenager or young adult. I am frequently questioned about it by young children as well as teenagers. "How important is it to set goals?" is a frequently asked question. I, for one, can certainly attest to the significance of goal-setting in my life, and I cannot overestimate how important it has always been and continues to be in one's journey toward discovering their purpose and unparalleled success.

In essence, setting goals is one of the few keys to success. It gives you a vivid image of where and who you want to be, once it is all said and done—your own road map.

Bottom line; if you are not one to set goals, start now, and don't stop until you achieve them.

Have you ever considered how your life might change if you made it a point to set milestones for yourself and work diligently toward achieving each one? It works like magic! Not only will you succeed in reaching your objectives, but there is also a rewarding feeling associated with completing a task that you set out to complete. To then be confident in your ability to complete personal goals responsibly.

What Are Goals?

To quote another expert on the subject, renowned speaker, and author Greg S. Reid;

12

"A dream written down with a date becomes a goal. A goal broken down into steps becomes a plan. A plan backed by action makes your dreams come true."

A goal is an objective, the focus of your aspirations, and the outcome you hope to achieve. It is impossible to overstate the importance of goal-setting in making your high school experience all the more fulfilling.

Goal-setting is fundamental to your progress as a student. It helps you gain perspective on your desired outcome. A man without a goal is comparable to someone traveling without a destination in mind. Such a person could very well end up lost. Without a goal or objective, you cannot thrive in this significant stage of your life. You must set goals that will distinguish you as a pacesetter if you intend to set the example for others to follow.

When I was a freshman in high school, Mrs. Taylor, the school counselor, asked each new student to write down the goals they hoped to accomplish throughout their years as high schoolers, during the freshman orientation on their first day. In my senior year, I was privileged to watch her do the same to the freshman class of 2019. Although, this time as the head boy. Goal-setting has the same effect today, as it did all those years ago. I have never met a successful person who claimed that they didn't have goals in mind when they started.

"Setting goals is the first step in transforming the invisible into the visible."
- Tony Robbins

There are few things more painful to hear as a high school student than discovering your parents might be on the brink of bankruptcy. Any teenager would be devastated to hear that. I became aware that my parents' finances were deteriorating at some point during my time in high school. At the time, I knew this could potentially throw me off and cause me to lose my concentration, but I decided against it. I was simply unable to let that experience shape who I would become. I made a commitment to myself that I would make the most of every penny spent on me and graduate from high school among the top students, and I followed through on that promise.

I envisioned myself receiving my diploma at my graduation ceremony, and it happened.

I believed that I had to have begun having a significant impact in the lives of many before I was legally considered an adult. I had no connections, there were no established platforms, and there were no resources. Today, my amazing team and I have connected with many young people worldwide through the platform Youngazu, which I founded.

Every time you set a goal for yourself, you are unknowingly improving your chances of realizing your aspirations.

Setting goals prepare you for what's ahead. A goal that is properly set is halfway achieved, according to the former author and WWII veteran, Zig Ziglar. Goals have the unique ability to increase your level of readiness because they enable you to visualize your ideal outcome. Society is urged by Stephen Covey to start each day with the end in mind. Begin every journey, like the one you are on right now, with a picture of the end in mind. Visualize where you want to be at the end of any journey, even before the journey starts.

Regardless of context or your goal, being class president, the head boy or head girl, valedictorian, prom king or queen, or even class clown, that works too. All you need to do is work toward that goal while maintaining a laser-like focus on it. You'll be inspired to keep going by that tunnel vision. You'll know there is only one direction to go: forward, in the direction of the light, in the direction of your objective.

One without a goal is like an archer who shoots aimlessly and blindly. The issue with not having a goal, according to Bill Copeland, is that you can spend your entire life running up and down the field without ever scoring. Do not be fooled by anyone. It's not "just how you're wired". You are not a failure or a moron! Simply stated, you are going in circles because you haven't carefully considered what you want to accomplish.

When you set a goal, even if you do not even achieve it, you are still on track, because you have a clear idea of what you want to accomplish, as opposed to when you do not. The context of that goal will then help you decide on the best course of action to take in various situations.

Hard work is required to achieve goals!

*"Focus, hard work is the real key to success. Keep your eyes on the goal, and just keep taking the next step towards completing it..." – **John Carmack***

The most important determinant of success is hard work! You've probably seen it in the hallways, in all of your classes, at the gym, and in books, and guess what, this one is no different. I've always believed in working hard, and I won't start saying otherwise now.

Success and hard work go hand in hand, and the latter is the only way to get the former. Without any effort, success is never within reach. The difficulty with hard work is that it necessitates perseverance and dedication, which is a problem for many. But to succeed, we must put in the work and be prepared to trust the process; one that has worked for many great men and women today.

Hard work is a virtue that has persisted for millennia. It can never be substituted. Just ask Thomas Edison; before creating the light bulb, he had 1,000 unsuccessful attempts. The success of Thomas Edison is proof that effort pays off. Of course, he rejoiced in his achievement, but more importantly, he saw earlier failures as "1,000 steps" to success rather than failures.

Working hard is the best investment you can make into your future. You cannot compare someone tenacious in pursuing a goal with someone who is not. The difference is as clear as night and day. The time to fight is right now. Struggle today for the pleasures of tomorrow. No one can work to achieve your goals on your behalf because you are the driving force behind them.
It will cost you a lot to work hard, but it will cost you even more if you fail to do so, and that will be most regrettable.

Making the most of your time in school should be your main goal as a student, and working hard to accomplish this is crucial. You and I know that failure to work hard is tantamount to actual failure.

Permit me to debunk this idea of 'FAIL' being the 'First Attempt In Learning'. No one likes failing at all. That is the reality of life! So why wait to fail the first time when you could have worked hard and gotten it right.

While failing is not a crime; it is not anyone's desire either so let us stop dignifying it. You have what it takes to achieve your goals and you must work hard to see to it that they are achieved. The only time you can call failure your "First Attempt In Learning" is after you have put in a lot of effort and most likely missed it. If you don't try, however, and things go wrong, it's because you simply didn't try at all. It's not too late for you to start acting responsibly and putting more effort into achieving your goals.

While the majority of the kids were having what they would consider "fun," I was working hard to contribute because there is no point in having fun today and suffering tomorrow. Did I enjoy it? Absolutely not. However, the silver lining is that I was successful in achieving my goal of excellence.

Identify your objectives and make every effort to achieve them. Work ethic pays off! You probably wouldn't be reading this if I had chosen to be one of the people who made a list of goals on orientation day and hid it in my closet. After all, where would I start? Giving away what you don't have is impossible.

Success remains the benefit of a hard day's work. It is impossible to overstate the value of working hard to accomplish your goals. Although it is difficult, as the name suggests, hard work does not cause death. You become more resilient as a result, and success more closely resembles you than you could have ever imagined.

Failure is not a crime, as I stated earlier, especially if you have worked hard to accomplish your goals. Since every mistake is an opportunity to learn, unlearn, and relearn something, I believe failure almost does not exist. When our plans for achieving our goals don't go as expected, we should, however, remain optimistic, reassess our strategies, and try using a different approach.

Take a Step Back, Restrategize and You'll See the Bigger Picture!

There will always be a point in your high school journey when you feel like you might never achieve your goals or that they don't seem as attainable as they used to. If you have been working so hard to win the award for best student, best actor, or best athlete of the year, you may be disappointed. You should be aware that there are ups and downs in life because it's not always a bed of roses. Being a failure in your own eyes is the worst thing you could possibly do to yourself because the world will not see you as a winner until you begin to treat yourself as one.

Failures are those who stumble and don't get back up. Failure to accomplish a goal does not preclude future success in that goal or other goals. It is merely a reminder for you to rethink your approach and keep trying. There is a reason you must rethink your strategy before making a second attempt. The definition of insanity, according to Albert Einstein, is repeating the same action and expecting a different outcome.

When a child is trying to walk, he gets up and falls, and when he repeats this, it is assumed that he is not even trying to walk. But everyone will be pleased with the child's progress once he reaches for something, puts his hand on that platform, and starts moving from one place to another.

Your strategy for accomplishing your goals must change if you want to succeed after making a mistake. Nothing will change or work if you keep doing things the same way; however, if you choose to approach that goal differently, you will succeed. How deliberately they pursue their objectives sets the most successful people apart from everyone else. And one of the best ways to be deliberate about achieving your goals is to constantly push yourself to do so by using a new approach.

Change, as the old saying goes, is a constant in life, so you have to accept that the way you did something yesterday might not work out today. If you are expecting the new, you cannot repeat the old. It is not done on purpose. Old goals that are yet to be successful require fresh approaches and ongoing encouragement to succeed.

Don't give up trying. You are well on your way to achieving your objectives when you specialize in the practice of repeatedly attempting things in various ways. "I will never stop trying and pursuing my goals because I am only headed for the top," declare this to yourself.

Draw Out A Plan!

Everybody wants great things for themselves, but they don't just happen to you; you have to work for them. The lack of a detailed plan to achieve goals is the main cause of goal failure.

Desiring to accomplish a goal is one thing, but planning how to do so is quite another. Take academic excellence as an example. If you want it, you must plan how to get it, rather than just having the goal in the first place. Goals require preparation!

I recall when Tolu Awoderu, a dear friend, was planning to launch Lantern Lessons, a Christian children's ministry. The vision first appeared on January 11th, but Lantern Lessons didn't begin until March. Imagine! The vision appeared three months later. She and her team continued to plan during that time. She probably did not want to start a project that she couldn't complete.

The Youngazu vision came on September 1, 2020, but we didn't hold our first webinar until October 3, 2020. We planned extensively during the time between when we came up with the webinar idea and when it actually took place. We had a lot of meetings, had to communicate with a lot of people, and wrote a lot of letters. We had a lot to do, and this allowed us to deal with setbacks on time. Our first "Youth Evolution!" webinar series was successful in part because of our careful planning. I could see if we had only distributed posters a week before the event. Wouldn't you describe that as insane? Yes, you would. As such, Plan accordingly right away!

Bar raisers live a lifestyle of planning. The sooner you turned planning into a way of life, the closer you'd be to realizing your objectives. Give me six hours to cut down a tree, and I'll spend the first four sharpening my ax, as Abraham Lincoln once said. The statement is self-explanatory.

You might find it interesting to know that Abraham Lincoln faced many difficulties in his role as President of the United States of America and that the majority of the choices he made have a significant impact, today on the country's current degree of sovereignty. Before making such decisions, he had to carefully plan; otherwise, the United States might not be what it is today. A nation is still affected by the planning of one man from yesterday. Thus, the significance of strategic planning.

Planning is dreaming. Gloria Steinem said that without leaps of imagination or dreaming, we lose the excitement of possibilities. After all, dreaming can be likened to planning. Essentially, every time we are encouraged to dream big, we are also subtly encouraged to plan big. Gloria is making this assertion. We can infer from Gloria's words that preparation opens the door to countless opportunities. One characteristic of humans is that, when we make plans, we always want to see them through to completion. It is organic! Therefore, your zeal would draw you to opportunities that you could take advantage of to accomplish your goal.

It is time for you to buckle up, buddy. Don't you think it's about time you did? You HAVE GOT to create a plan to realize your dreams. Be deliberate. It is simpler to stick to a plan and work toward your goals than it is to keep going in circles.

On To The Next One: Learn to Set New Goals!

The worst thing you can ever do to yourself in goal setting is to be conceited. Every day, the world changes, and while you struggle to rise to the top, others are doing the same. As much as you would love to excel, others yearn to do the same day and night. Thus, after achieving some goals, you cannot afford to become complacent.

Goals are not unalterable. They must be continuously modified until they are realized. The meaning of being ALIVE is being able to ADAPT. There is something more profound about it than eating, sleeping, or reproducing. The true essence of LIFE is the capacity to EVOLVE and the wisdom to know WHEN to do so to make the most of any circumstance. This is what it means to be ALIVE. Consider a hunter, who set out to kill a buck, but despite his best efforts, had not seen one in several hours. There is no way our hunter would leave empty-handed. He must therefore reevaluate the situation, modify his original goal, or decide to kill a boar rather than a buck.

Each day is a mystery waiting to be unraveled. As there are so many unknowns in life, you should cultivate your ability to adapt. You must continually reevaluate your objectives and, after refining the ones you already have set new ones. You will need to set goals as long as you remain on Earth. You should earn your keep by consistently setting these things as goals because you will always want to accomplish new things every time. From wanting to arrive at biology class a little earlier than the day before, to wanting to turn in your projects earlier than every other student. Those are goals, and as trivial as they may seem, they remain objectives that must be met.

When you start setting new goals, you will be a candidate for ongoing standard-setting. Bar raisers are known for constantly setting goals, but you have to be very deliberate about it. Keep setting new goals to create new mountains for yourself to climb because climbing those mountains makes you a bar-raiser!

When you set new goals, your mind is strengthened to take on new challenges and you remain psychologically alert? Let's look at that closely: You set one goal in your mind, and then you set another. It keeps you on your toes, ready for the next challenge because your mind will be constantly active.

Set SMART goals!

Although setting new goals and goals in general, is a good thing, we must remember that goal-setting must be done wisely. Setting new objectives when they are not necessary at that time will be foolish on your part. You will simply keep changing your targets while missing your shots.

The more compelling a case there is for you to set smart goals.

'SMART goals' have received a lot of attention in recent years. Most especially, in the K-12 system. As a result, I won't bore you with an explanation of what SMART goals are, because I'm sure you already have an idea; instead, I'll highlight some important points. — Yes, despite the pre-stated fact, there are still a few things you should know about setting SMART goals. Did you think I was going to end the chapter there?

- **Specific goals** – Your goals should be clearly defined. You need to know what you want exactly and not beat around the bush. For example, 'I want to have a 4.0 GPA at the end of my junior year, to increase my chances of getting into my desired college'.

- **Measurable goals** – Any objective you set should be measurable using a set of standards. To gauge the extent of your progress, you should set goals that can be tracked. It is measurable to say, "By the end of the month, I want to increase my savings by 5%."

- **Achievable goals** – When you take into account where you are right now, your goals ought to be simple for you to achieve. Setting a goal that you know will be impossible for you to accomplish is not a good idea. Consider this; "I will read a chapter of my Chemistry textbook once a week."

- **Relevant goals** – Your objectives must be compatible with where you are in the academic process. You can't now decide that you want to build a house because that is not in the picture yet. The statement "I want to score 1400 on my SAT" relates to your status as a student.

- **Time-bound goals** – Every objective requires a deadline that you intend to meet. It supports your commitment to achieving that objective. "I want to be prepared for my exams by the end of the fifth week", would be a good time-bound objective.

SMART goals have proven to be highly effective especially when you set them, and follow them up. Your goals should satisfy the above criteria. They should be specific in action, measurable by criteria, achievable by your capacity, relevant to your being a student, and of course, timely to meet deadlines. With these, you are covered, and you have booked a seat for yourself at the top.

Don't Dive In, Be Tactical In Your Approach

After setting your goals, you must be tactical in your approach to achieving them. We have looked at planning how to achieve our goals, but we need to ensure that we are tactical even with our plans.

We already know that the whole process of achieving our goals is not a walk in the park. Tactics and strategies will make you get to the top faster than you can ever imagine. Tactics help you defy protocols. They give you an edge over others and will make you unique amongst your peers.

For my entire stay in high school and even up till now, tactics have always helped me in all that I do. Instead of reading textbooks to prepare for an exam the next day, a tactical student will use study guides, and questions from tests and will only study what he finds difficult to understand.

If you continue to go about things the way everyone goes about them, you will remain a regular person for the rest of your life but if you do things differently, you are going to stand out. It's just the trade of

During the COVID-19 lockdown, I decided to start working out daily. I set a goal for myself to do sixty push-ups every day. Now, I was out of shape, and I DEFINITELY could not do thirty push-ups all at once (I still can't) so here is what I did – I decided that I will do twenty push-ups in the morning, twenty in the afternoon, and another twenty in the evening. That way, I was able to reach the target I had set for myself and from then I became used to it.

Watch students who do exceptionally well, they don't study the way others do. There is a process to it. They listen attentively in class because that is where most of the salient points are dropped by teachers. They also refer to past tests and quizzes, and they have personal notes to record discoveries in various classes and topics. They are assertive and always eager to know more. THAT is being tactical! So, when some other students are studying hard trying to cram in a semester's worth of information within a week, they already have seventy percent of the syllabus in their heads and will prepare for the remaining thirty percent.

You will need to be tactical to get to the top and even more tactical to REMAIN at the top. Never undermine the value of strategies in getting you to your chosen destination. Traffic has never been (and will never be) a good excuse to be late to an interview. You can always work around it, by being tactical–leave home earlier or find a quicker route! Do not remain in the traffic! There are smarter ways to excel and you must take advantage of them.

Blue Skies!

The joy you get when you achieve your goals can not be compared to anything else. The fulfillment it gives you is beautiful. You can achieve your goals if you are willing to put in place what is necessary to get them accomplished.

So, it is time for you to reach for the stars. That should be your goal and I know you will achieve even greater because you are limitless. I pray that whatever you set your mind to achieve will be achieved because you are an achiever.

CHAPTER 3

o · · · · · · · · o

THE VALUE YOU GIVE
YOURSELF

"Values are like fingerprints. Nobody's the same, but you leave them all over everything you do"
*— **Elvis Presley***

YOU ARE SPECIAL. This would be true if we all embraced ONE. SIMPLE. FACT— we aren't.

As human beings, we are SPECIAL, but as an individual, ARE YOU SPECIAL?

Being truly special carries such weight that it cannot be expressed to someone simply for existing. Such a prestigious title does not come easily.

What makes an individual special is not innate. Therefore, no one is born special. The value you place on yourself is what truly distinguishes you as a unique person.

Ultimately, the value you place on yourself determines what you share with the rest of the world. It is a gift that keeps on giving and is helpful to both you and the environment. It determines how far you will advance in life. To this end, you must instill exemplary qualities, standards, and virtues in yourself.

It is a known fact that our world has gradually become very corrupt and that the values that previous generations once upheld are vanishing. Today's world is perverse because of the rise of technology and the new wave of ideologies propagated by television, movies, and generally the whole advent of pop culture.

The world has completely changed. For protection, people did not need to carry pocket knives and pepper spray as we do now. Strangers might offer to assist you, and you might reciprocate. The very values and standards that kept our society together have indeed been lost to our generation, but there is good news: you and I can bring them back! How? by fostering the proper values within us.

As a child, I was taught that values are the accepted norms, behaviors, ideas, and principles that society appreciates and seeks. Wherever you are, your values help you stand out. These are the guiding principles that you must follow throughout your time in high school and beyond. If you don't consistently live by the right moral principles, it will be difficult for you to succeed.

The loss of gold is much,

The loss of time is more,

The loss of honor is such a loss.

That no man can restore.

The loss of honor is incomparable to the majority of the things we value highly. Keep it together! When you are a person of little or no virtue, there is a lot at stake in life. Give yourself a lot of value. Create a persona for yourself that others can stand up for even when you are not there. Ask yourself, "Am I on the right track?" today. Do I possess the proper values? Am I deserving of admiration?

If you are unable to directly respond to these inquiries, you should reflect on your actions and search within.

A Good Reputation is Preferable to Great Wealth

I once heard about a man who spent many years working for a multinational corporation but ended up with little to nothing in return. His daughter had renounced him as her father, claiming that he despised her so much that he didn't leave her an inheritance. She decided to break off contact with him, but not before he assured her that what he had left for her went beyond substantial wealth.

He died alone, as was to be expected, and was buried in a rather shoddy manner. His daughter visited his former place of employment after the funeral, in search of employment. Because of her last name, the company chairman asked her during the interview whose daughter she was. In response, she stated her father's full name. The man exhaled in surprise and immediately informed her that they required a Managing Director and that he would like her to fill that position.

He told her that her father was an incredibly honorable man who would never accept money that was not due to him. He continued by saying that given her background and the fact that her father was always wary of anything that might damage his reputation, he thought she would run the business successfully. The young woman sobbed bitterly as she sat in her chair, remembering her father's final words to her before she left him. She was only able to enjoy that grace because of her father's reputation.

A solid reputation is very valuable. Anyone can benefit from the bliss that it brings at any time, anywhere. You're not too young to have your name inscribed in gold; in fact, it begins right now.

Every parent delights in watching their kids succeed and uphold an honorable name. Consider this: Pattie Mallette, Justin Bieber's mother, would not have had a story to include in "Nowhere but up" if Justin had lived a chaotic life. A thief's father will never be proud to refer to his child as a thief. The advice my mother gave me helped me get through high school, among other things. She would always assure my brother and me that she would never be present if any of us had a problem at school that required her presence because she could not bear to have children who would bring shame to her name.

Those words started to stick with me, and thankfully they helped to direct my behavior throughout my time in high school and even in life, generally. Always take the time to consider how your actions will affect your reputation before acting. Avoid doing it if it will cast doubt on your morals and judgment.

A positive reputation will leave a lasting impression on people, which will become your legacy. Don't you find it interesting that some names of people who lived more than a century ago are still used today?

Consider this: What will people associate you with when they hear your name in a few years? We all lay in our bed according to how we make it, so start doing it right, today.

A worthy image

You can see a reflection of yourself when you stand in front of a mirror. Your decision to improve your appearance or not will depend on the impression you create. Perhaps the picture you see shows your hair not pulled back neatly or your shirt collar not properly positioned; you will probably do something to fix it because you want to look good. Your outlook on life should be like that. Wherever you are, you should make an effort to present a positive image of yourself.

Never conform to negative trends; instead, be unique and authentic. There are tales of students who perform admirably at first but later change their ways. In the name of Jesus, your situation will never be that dire; however, you must be dedicated to making sure that you always conduct yourself with integrity and high moral standards. It is in your best interest to consciously turn a new leaf in any area of your life where there is cause for concern rather than disguising yourself as a good person. No one can truly conceal their true nature for all time.

The way one person perceives you greatly influences how other people will perceive you. We had a new PE teacher when I was in the 8th grade and I remember that one of the students was rude to him in the first lesson. "First impressions matter," he said in reference to her. Believe me when I say that the girl who had insulted him never had it easy during the time that teacher was employed at the school. The teacher always saw her through the lens of the self-image she had developed earlier, and soon both other teachers and students began to perceive the girl through the lens of a rude, truculent, and supercilious student when in reality, she was just a regular student who was being naughty.

First impressions are important. Gone are the days when people listened to your side of the story before they formed an opinion about you, so it is best you do not create a negative story for yourself at all. We see how people are dragged every day on social media for little mistakes. Every day on social media, we observe how people are shamed for insignificant errors. Remember that social media is an open platform, so anything posted there has a ripple effect and sticks in people's minds. Never forget that you can always make amends for your mistakes and create an admirable reputation for yourself.

You alone will benefit from the positive attention a respectable reputation garners. Carve your image into rocks so it will last forever. Because life doesn't end with high school, look beyond today. Create a persona for yourself that will leave a lasting impression on history. Create a reputation that elevates you.

If you're a soccer fan and you watched the 2020 Euros, you'll probably agree that it produced some moments that will go down in history and won't be easily forgotten. The post-game press conference by Cristiano Ronaldo is one of these crucial moments. Just before he started answering questions, he made a decision that cost Coca-Cola $4 billion. He chose to place a bottle of water in the camera's field of view rather than a bottle of Coke. A major corporation like Coca-Cola suffered a staggering 4 billion dollar loss as a result of that one act.

Imagine if Ronaldo were an average Joe at the mall. You most definitely would not care about his actions, let alone try to emulate them. So, friend, declare this with me and make sure it becomes one of your guiding principles: "I choose to develop a respectable reputation for myself."

Strong moral principles pay!

I once saw a video of a homeless poor man by Dhar Mann before. He was a street dweller who begged for alms from every person who passed him. A nice lady gave him a dollar one fateful day, and unbeknownst to her, her pricey wedding ring fell into the cup with the cash. The man examined the cash and was touched by the woman's kindness in giving him a full dollar. He was grateful for her generosity.

The man was able to recall that the nice lady had a ring on her finger and reasoned that she must have accidentally dropped it when he later found a ring in the cup. He started looking for his peculiar benefactor as a result, but in vain. During one of those searches, he made a stop at a shop to determine the ring's worth in case he wanted to sell it. The shop owner informed the beggar that he would purchase it from him for $4,000. The shop owner was eager to purchase the ring, so he immediately pulled out stacks of $100 bills and set them on the counter.

The poor man then turned to look at the ring and the cash. Something didn't seem right. Was he prepared to sell his morals for only $4,000? No, he could not possibly compromise his integrity by doing so. In an effort to find the woman, he stormed out of the store with more zeal than ever before. Fortunately, he found her in her office. The woman, who had been moved to pity, even questioned him about why he had brought the ring back when he could have simply sold it.

After that, the woman's friend advised her to launch a GoFundMe to help the man find housing. As luck would have it, the man's story touched many people, and more than $100,000 was raised, allowing him to purchase a home rather than continue to rent one. Well, that's how lucrative a person with high standards typically finds their life to be.

Integrity makes a person stand out from the crowd. Such people never have an easy time fitting in; instead, they stand out because they are unable to participate in the quirks of troublemakers. You are also capable of being that. While there is no reward for blending in, those who stand out eventually attract attention.

Many people have narrowly avoided death, and their only saving grace was a simple set of guiding principles they had committed to upholding. I recall watching a movie about a young man whose friends intended to poison him. In addition to God, the only thing that saved him was the promise he had made to himself that he would not consume any alcoholic beverages. As a result, when his friends poisoned his drink and even urged him to take at least a sip, he simply poured it out when they left the room.

You must always possess the right habits and traits if you want to be successful. If there is one quality I hold in high regard in any relationship I am in, it is honesty. I make it clear at the outset of every relationship that I detest dishonesty because it has an unrivaled ability to ruin things. It will be in my best interest to live up to the standard I have set for myself, which is to never make friends with dishonest people. Setting a principle is one thing; living by it is quite another.

Live by it!

What is the first thing you'll ask a friend who approaches you and says he wants to start exercising every day? "Will you be able to keep up?" That is going to be the first thing you ask. You are not asking that question because you think your friend's sudden decision is bad, but rather because you care that he not only begins the new lifestyle but adheres to it. After all, only then will he be able to benefit from it.

Declaring that you will be a disciplined student is not sufficient. You receiving discipline is what makes a difference. Many students are unable to adhere to predetermined standards. Peers, the environment, and other unimportant factors have a big impact on them. Since the art of retaining success requires highly principled people, it will be difficult for you to be successful if you are the type who easily strays from established principles.

I once had the pleasure of going to a tutorial center and meeting a young boy there. When I questioned him about a group of older boys I thought were annoying, he responded, "Most of the guys you see here are very unserious. They would leave class whenever they showed up and head to a nearby field to drink, smoke, and flirt with girls. I asked him jokingly, "What about you, are you not one of them?" after being shocked. God forbid! he grinned as he said to me. I am aware of why I am here. I came here to learn, and since learning is my main goal, I can never get involved in what they do.

How many students in this generation possess such intelligence? We now hear of high school students hooking up, smoking, drinking, and committing crimes involving firearms. Even more perplexing is the fact that some of these students come from decent homes. Do not ever allow anyone to have a bad influence on you, please. Be grateful for who you are, and only strive to meet high standards.

Listen to your conscience! All humans have a small, non-physical component called a "conscience" that acts as a gatekeeper for the majority of our actions. So before you make most of your decisions, let your conscience start to weigh them. Do not, my friend, what you would like to do now but know you will regret doing in ten years. Don't do anything that you know you shouldn't do in front of your parents or teachers. Don't do anything you intend to do that you know they will disapprove of. As you can see, there is never a good reason to do something bad, so refrain from doing it!

The school is one of the few places where we can begin disinfecting the world because it is already too polluted. Participate in the sanitizers. You can only be a member of the sanitizers by refusing to follow the norms of society.

Do not conform! Say NO to everything that will want you to conform but renew your mind every day so that you can show what is acceptable. A man once said that it is foolishness to be ashamed of something gainful. Though it is tough; the right lifestyle pays anytime and anywhere so do not be ashamed of it.

A while back, I watched a Dhar Mann video clip. It featured a young boy who was labeled a "nerd" in high school. At a party, some guys—the so-called "cool kids"—invited him to drink and smoke, but he politely declined. With the way he was living his life, they warned him that he would never amount to anything in life. As luck would have it, a few years later, the man was about to get into his Porsche when he noticed the same group of men approaching his vehicle. They were astounded to learn that while they had accomplished nothing, their nerdy friend had become a success. They then started to feel bad about what they had done. Regret is demeaning. I hope you never experience it.

Many people will be prevented from reaching the stars by their inability to consistently maintain the proper lifestyle, not anything major. I certainly am not perfect, but I made a promise to never let anyone find me lacking in my academic performance, and it has continued to benefit me. Was it simple? Oh no! Even though it is simpler to steal money than to work hard for it, the rewards are very different. When caught, a thief will become punished and disgraced, but a genuine earner will always be praised.

Stop blaming others for your problems and start taking responsibility for your own actions. You are to blame for all your wrongdoings. Bill Gates once said that while being born poor is not your fault, dying poor is.

Be zealous about following your principles. By doing this, you uphold your honor and elevate your value. Instead of just saying it, live it! Don't just say, "I won't cheat," actually do it! Don't just say, "I won't be lazy," actually do it!

A Fresh Start Is Very Much In View!

Change is the only thing that is constant in life. The old life that wasn't profitable vanishes when change takes hold. It's time for you to turn a new leaf so that you can be translated into someone for whom others are praying and live a fruitful life. You can obtain it. Before anything can be new, all things must first die. Meetings between the new and the old are not permitted because doing so would result in an unhealthy conflict of interest. For the other to rule, the first must yield.

One method for implementing a new system in an organization is to run it concurrently with the current one, but this method is less efficient than others and very expensive. A ship cannot be commanded by two captains without risking capsize. In a similar vein, you decide to take your studies more seriously while still skipping class or submitting assignments after the deadline. The choice of which lifestyle will give way to the other is entirely up to you. One lifestyle must make way for the other to take root.

Interestingly, often people who tend to reconsider their former lifestyles and let go of the negative aspects of their lives tend to become more effective individuals. When I was in high school, there was a particular boy in my set that was quite sound, academically, but he was not among the top students. As soon as we got to senior high school, it was almost as if something had entered him. He became among the top students in the set and even graduated as one of the best.

Now is the time to decide. With a pen and a piece of paper, make a list of all the things you are doing that prevent you from being an A-class person. Then, write down how you intend to stop doing each of these things. You need to free yourself from the hold of the activities you are engaging in that are not positively benefiting you. Except for you, no one else can choose to give you a new beginning.

You should act now! You need to deal with the triggers of whatever you are doing that is wrong. For instance, you are the kind that does not study, and you know that the cause of this is that you spend hours on your phone, or you are always gaming, or worse still, your chores take a lot of your time, and you end up with little time to do your assignments. Then, you need to ensure that you put that phone down.

There was a time I felt I was getting too engrossed with my phone, and I contemplated giving it to a teacher to keep for and from me during school days until Friday evenings after school. It sounds crazy, I know. Sometimes, crazy decisions translate into unexplainable excellence.

You can cut down on the time you spend playing those video games. They can help one become more intelligent, but if they are used improperly, they can also cause brain drain. You must prioritize your chores, make sure that you complete them all by the deadline, and refrain from putting them off.

You will need to make some unconventional choices and follow through on them, but keep in mind that you stand to benefit from the entire process of change. Whatever is profitable, as far as I'm concerned, merits genuine sacrifice. You might notice that some of your friends may start to drift away the day you start evolving and becoming a new person. You should be grateful that they are gone because they were never the right fit for you and their departure frees you up to move forward.

Three Values that count!

There are three fundamental standards that I believe every student must adhere to. These standards have yielded results in my life. They helped me all through my journey in high school and I will be glad to share them with you.

- **Diligence** – A lazy man cannot eat, according to an African proverb. That clarifies the meaning of diligence, in my opinion. The importance of hard work cannot be overstated; it is one of the virtues that the world honors. Your main goal as a student is to receive an education that will enable you to contribute to society as a useful and accountable member. This can only be possible if you put in a lot of effort. Keep in mind that the common denominator in the stories of people who dropped out but succeeded anyway is always hard work.

  The quality of your yield will depend on how well you use what you already have.

  Start being accountable to yourself and taking control of some aspects of your life. The ability to raise responsible students is one of the benefits of boarding schools. You don't need to be reminded to do your laundry in the hostel. If you don't, your clothes will smell, and you'll look bad. Last but not least, perseverance grows you, not kills you. Stop waiting for your parents to tell you to read, sleep, or even eat, and start taking care of yourself. You are a young adult now, not a child, and maturing isn't determined solely by the words you say, but also by what you do.

- **Integrity will stand you out** – Integrity can serve as the comparative advantage you have over others; can people vouch for you? The ability to have your 'Yes' be 'Yes' and your 'No' be 'No' is essential in putting you at the zenith of wherever you are.

  Integrity is upholding moral principles. It is the capacity to stick out as the only person on the right side when everyone else chooses to do the opposite. Being an honest person can be challenging because almost everyone will think you're foolish, but don't change! Never feel guilty for doing what is right. Your peers might very well put your integrity to the test, but only choose those who share your principles and values to avoid being corrupted or tempted into doing something you'll later regret.

Integrity will pay you more than silver and gold. Shelly Francis once said; that a meaningful life of integrity requires courage.

- **Commitment and dedication** – The difference between best and second-best is simply the extra effort put in. The one-hour extra study time invested works wonders. As a student, your primary constituency is your education, so you must dedicate your time to excelling as a student, an athlete, or at anything else. The sacrifice parents make for their children's education is by no means a cinch. The principal of my school stated that the total cost per student for our parents to support us through high school for six years was approximately thirty-six thousand dollars in a meeting with the seniors and their parents. So, picture yourself in the position of your parents, incurring such expenses only to have your child struggle academically. How would you react?

Do not play around! Know that you are in school for a reason, and it is not forever; so be committed to making the best of your stay. Make it one to remember. You need to be steadfast in ensuring you are successful. That is the only way to engender progress at any level. No one works wonders more than a committed and dedicated person because the person has a 'By all means' mentality to achieving his goals. That is the mentality you need as a student. The mentality that you must ace your tests and exams. Note that the end justifies the means so if in achieving your goal you engage in what you should not, it will always show itself; so, refrain from it.

Excellence requires hard work and moral character. They take you to the top. However, maintaining that top spot then requires a commitment to the values and guidelines that got you there. Commitment is what differentiates. It sets you apart from the rest. It makes you the best, and the person you're ahead of, second-best

Friend, you become valuable when you have principles. You gain enormous significance and become well-known for that special gift only you can give the world.

CHAPTER 4

o · · · · · · · · o

ATTITUDE DETERMINES
YOUR ALTITUDE

"Your attitude, not your aptitude, will determine your altitude."
– Zig Ziglar

A good attitude is an asset. It can help clear paths that seem difficult to tread, which is an advantage for you as a student. Many students fail because of their attitudes; it is a sum of who you are and what you stand for. It represents you before people get to know you and creates the first impression you make on others.

It is one thing to be highly principled with the morals you uphold; it is another to have a good attitude. Your attitude is like a mirror of your values. Does it shock you sometimes that a new teacher acts nicer or stricter to you than to other students in the same class? Well, they might have heard about you from a previous teacher- the more reason you should behave appropriately at all times.

Many people have received unusual favors because of their attitude. You see, no two humans are the same; not even a set of twins, or people of the same tribe, race, age, or gender. So you need to have an attitude that brings you good fortune, instead of one that is a point of concern.

You should watch your attitude consciously because it can make or mar you! Don't let people get negative opinions about you because you put up a character that is not yours. Oh! Are you surprised that I said "it is not yours?" **Friend, no negative character is yours. It is only a habit that you have cultivated over time and find difficult to let go of.** It is also one of the devil's antics to portray you as a horrible person so that he can accuse you before our God (Revelation 12:10).

The three-fold character builder

Someone said, "Watch your thoughts, they become your words. Watch your words, they become your actions. Watch your actions, they become your character. Watch your character, it becomes your destiny." You can see now what happens before you form your character. Hence, you should take caution.

Remember that the heart is the core of all issues concerning life. So you are to keep that heart with all diligence. You should purify your heart because it holds the root of the person you will become. If you have listened to criminals confess, you will realize that more than seventy-five percent of crimes are well-thought-out beforehand.

The devil comes to sow evil seeds in people's minds, but you must understand that your body is the temple of the Most High, and the Holy Spirit will help you. Think positively and channel your thoughts into building a character worthy of emulation. You will eventually speak out about what your heart contains. If your heart is good, you will speak good, and if it is evil, you will speak evil.

The tongue is designed to work in synchrony with the heart. Watch your tongue. I often tell people that not everything in your mind is worth speaking out about. Some things are better left unsaid. Note that words are like eggs and once they land, you cannot take them back. So be chaste with your words. Someone I know often says, "God knows how powerful the tongue is, so He guards it with thirty-two soldiers and has made two padlocks to keep it shut." Words are potent enough to create or destroy. Don't forget that words were used for creation - God said, "let there be light," and there was light. They can also be used for destruction.

When your thoughts and speeches are geared towards positivity, you will easily achieve great exploits since it is the last fold of the character formation process. The deeds of great men live on always, so be passionate about championing causes that will outlive you instead of being a mischief-maker.

Stand out with character!

How does it feel to be alone in a line when there's another queue with many people in it? Awkward or Cool? Being bold when doing the right thing and living the right way is one of the most precious gifts you could ever give yourself. It is tough to be alone on the right path, but it pays in the end.

Setting great goals is never enough; be intelligent and smart, diligent and talented. A good attitude complements all the exceptional qualities any individual can possess. I would rather work with an upright person whose character is 'worthy of emulation' than an intelligent person who lacks good character. Your attitude is like candlelight; it can never be hidden. It always has a way of revealing itself, so you should be on your best behavior at all times.

An African proverb vehemently states that "Charity begins at home but does not end there." That statement explains the fact that you can never conceal your character. It follows you everywhere. It is your shadow; it never leaves you. It shows itself even when you try covering it up, so an admirable character is advantageous.

Let people, both old and young, aspire to have your type of personality. Create shoes that will be too large for whoever finds themselves in your position. I have seen several people come up to me to tell me how much I inspire them and how they yearn to be like me. I become astonished when I hear these statements because subconsciously, I know there is a better version of myself that I always strive towards.

Four - Six Years in High School

Depending on what part of the world you live in, you spend four to six years in high school. Those years should be exploits-making, pacesetting, trailblazing, bar-raising years; not years of having the school report your misconduct to your parents. You should not have your parents sit before the principal, listening to how you bullied a fellow student, disrespected a school staff, or engaged in examination malpractice or some immoral act. You must set the pace for others to follow.

Be the light that illuminates others. Whatever action you cannot take in front of your parents is pointless. Don't even think about it. Before you involve yourself in destructive acts, consider the efforts and resources your parents (or sponsors) have put into your education. I believe it should restrain you from doing anything that will make others question your dignity.

The nature of a unique person is celebratory. Thus, if your peculiarity is not worth celebrating and doesn't birth excellence, it is abnormal because distinction and celebration cohere. These two things must be evident for you to have a breathtaking quality.

36

I promised myself never to be the reason why the school management would summon my parents concerning misbehavior. How could I think of bothering them with such nonsense? My parents never had the time, anyway. My mum worked exhaustively at the bank to see us through school. It would have been irresponsible of me to become that unserious.

Funny enough, my mother had made it clear to my brother and I that if the school ever invited her over for a punishable act, she would not show up and would eventually withdraw that child from school because she could not afford to waste resources. My friend, don't waste resources but use them to your advantage.

From the start, that warning had stuck with me. It followed me everywhere and is still with me today. I received my first award in high school in October 2014. I had just joined the school and was the best writer in the school's book week for that year. I was the first student amongst my peers to win an award of excellence. I started well and continued the same till the end.

Be the student that radiates excellence, and not the one who is a heartache to his loved ones. Standing out of the crowd is challenging, but fruitful. Nothing in life pays more than being unique.

Be yourself: Don't fake it!

Do not "fake it till you make it". People do not like pretenders. If you are not who you seem to be, your true self will eventually surface, no matter how much you try to hide it. A Leopard cannot hide its spots.

Posing to be who you are not is the worst thing you can ever do to yourself. Pretense robs you of many things. Let people know you for who you are and not for who you claim to be. Do not ever fake your identity.

I heard the story of a man who faked his attitude in a job interview. Naturally, he was an unruly, haughty individual but during the assessment, he claimed to be meek and calm. The employers granted him the job, where he successfully kept up with his pretentious attitude for about two weeks. Before long, the young man revealed his true colors and bungled. His behavior was so bad, that he didn't last a month in the organization. Sometimes others find it difficult to believe that a certain person would do evil, simply because they seem incapable of wrongdoing. But I always tell people – "Whatever somebody does in secrecy will come to the open one day." Dear reader, the same principle applies to one's character. Any negative behavior you think you can conceal will eventually reveal itself - perhaps in the worst manner possible. Why not do away with it early enough?

James Russell Lowell said, "Sincerity is impossible unless it pervades the whole being, and the pretense of it saps the very foundation of character." For you to be one-hundred-percent original, you must allow genuineness to consume you completely. You would get to a level where people reference your lifestyle because of how plain you are. That point should be your goal.

Hypocrites never get celebrated, and even if they do, they hardly last because their crooked ways catch up with them faster than they can imagine. You are still young and prone to making mistakes. These mistakes mold you, and older people and guardians in your life can correct you based on these wrongdoings.

Right now, you are at a stage where you shouldn't worry about putting up the perfect image. Friend, foolishness dwells in the heart of a child, so you don't have to want to portray yourself as who you are not.

Another thing is peer pressure. You should never feel the need to follow every fad that comes your way. Our world is plagued with lots of pointless ideas called 'trends,' and not every one of them is worth trying. You should constantly remind yourself that you are God's temple and crafted for excellence before involving in any of these acts. Don't fool yourself into becoming what you are not all for the sake of doing "what's in vogue."

I remember back in ninth grade, most of my male friends enjoyed discussing football a lot. I never was a sports enthusiast, so most of the time, I would sit in their midst, not understanding or engaging in their arguments about games, teams, and players. One fateful day, I said to myself "Charles, it's high time you learned to speak the language of football."

When I got home that day, I tuned in to the sports channel on the television and started observing the ongoing football match. I even got a pen and paper and began jotting the stats and every other information I could read on the screen. I was determined to understand the dynamics of football, so I would participate actively in the boys' discussion at school the following day. The next day came and when the boys gathered to debate the previous day's events, I sat confidently, prepared to speak the 'football language' with them.

To my amazement, a dear friend noticed and said to me, "Charles, when did you become a football fan? You don't have to join us if you are not interested in sports. You can just sit with us." I was stupefied. It turned out to be one of the best pieces of advice I have ever received. And that was it for me.

To date, sports do not interest me, but I do not act otherwise. I could take part in them for recreation but not actively. Still, I celebrate those who enjoy sports and those who excel in them.

That is the 'Being Yourself' spirit! One with which you appreciate others for something but not necessarily try to be like them; because you know you are unique in your way. Imagine if I had kept on pretending till now. As funny as it sounds, I would still be writing football match stats on paper. I would have been taking a wrong step and probably wouldn't write this book today. But I chose to be original, and I will forever be grateful for my decision.

Let your character do the talking

Some people take too much pride in themselves instead of allowing their character to precede them. In your journey through high school, one of the greatest advantages you will have is when your character speaks for you. It will profit you greatly, and you have to work deliberately towards building it. One thing common to every bar-raiser is that they speak less of themselves and let people do the talking.

You would agree with me that a die-hard Messi fan speaks so much about Messi than he would himself. An educator once said to me, "In life, let people make the noise for you while you sit back." Now, don't forget that you cannot reap what you did not sow. Simply put, if you desire to have people celebrate your character and how wonderful you are, you must start building yourself from now.

You can use two adjectives to describe a popular person – Famous, and Notorious. Let me explain: "Famous" describes someone beloved for his good deeds, while notorious refers to someone who is known for his bad deeds. It is that simple. Now, ask yourself; what do you want to be acknowledged as? You must make your choice and stick to it. I made that decision years ago, and today, it has taken me to places I never thought I would reach.

High school for you doesn't have to be as stressful and problematic as people make it seem. It only becomes so when you let it. Many youths want

want freedom- they want to live their lives and go through school as they wish. If your parents had also chosen to live life negligently, perhaps you will not be where you are today.

In life, you are free but without liberty. Life will always present you with opportunities for advancement or retrogression, but your chosen path depends on you. Your character also will influence the decisions you make, so guard your heart with all diligence. Many honored men have fallen because of their attitude.

An arrogant, wealthy man will become poor one day. A poor man who is too proud can never be rich. Those who excel follow instructions, and one of those instructions is; "let your character do the talking so you don't have to talk too much."

If Abraham had been rude and unaccommodating to the strange men, they would have walked away with their message from God.

Michal's attitude made her the only barren woman in the whole of Israel, even after the Lord had promised, "There shall be none barren in the land." One's character can make God go back on his promises concerning their life and let them miss their place in glory. Be cautious! Even Jesus said to the seventy disciples that whenever they went anywhere to preach, they should turn their backs and stop preaching there if they were treated with scorn.

Your character says everything about you. One hundred percent. We all know about the 'Attitude calculator' that adds the numerical values of the alphabets in the word 'Attitude.' When you sum them up, you get a hundred. Your character is everything. I have said it and won't stop saying it. A man's character can promote him and at the same time bring him down to nothing. It is simply a function of what he desires.

You know yourself better than anyone, and so if your character is questionable and has never brought you any good, you know it, and it is time to change it. Anybody can have a fresh start if they will. Always remember that a good character increases your worth. So it is always a worthy cause.

Don't give what you can't take

Jesus stated clearly in Luke 6:31 that we should do unto others, what we want to be done unto us. In clearer terms, whatever we cannot take, we should refrain from dishing out. Long before I wrote this book, whenever I got angry, I would say mean and hurtful things to whoever had vexed me. This behavior cost me several precious relationships.

I want you to see it this way – I am upset, so I am not in my normal state, but the person I am facing is sober. Whatever I say or do to that person will mean something to them. People call it 'an angry frame of mind,' so if I hurt another person, I am only pouring out my anger. Now, that's where many of us get it wrong.

The individual at the receiving end will never see it that way. You bruised his pride and crushed his ego. You have made that person a shadow of himself. You have broken him into pieces, and it will take the grace of God for him to recover. Ever since I began weighing my words before speaking and reflecting on my actions, I have built lasting bonds with exceptional people. This change has contributed to the good network I enjoy today. I am surrounded by people who share similar ideas with me and are committed to my success. You can do it too. All you need to do is avoid giving people what you cannot take.

Your words are a fundamental part of your character. Be careful what you say and how you speak. You see, God knows how powerful the tongue is. Remember, there's the power of life and death in the tongue (Proverbs 18:21). So, God guarded it with thirty-two soldiers to protect it from speaking incautiously and then a padlock outside to control it. Friend, you are responsible for whatever you say. Every careless word translates into a reckless character, which will develop into a misplaced destiny. Do not toy with your destiny.

I see no reason why you should say to someone, something that you know will hurt you too. Many have killed people with their tongues. The tongue is such a powerful tool, it can define you if you allow it. But, no matter how much power the tongue wields, you still control it and what comes out of it.

Many people come off as having bad attitudes, not because they are bad people, but because their tongues have sold them out as such.

Not Everyone Can Handle What You Can

There is another category of people that feel that 'if they can take it, they can give it.' I believe you shouldn't throw anything at people just because you can tolerate it. I had some funny friends in high school whom we used to take turns, calling each other names occasionally. Although, we mostly saw them as jokes and felt they were normal; some of us couldn't handle it when such words were used on them. I even had a close friend who would surf the internet for different insults and write them down so he could use them at school the next day. Imagine such a level of nonchalance.

I had an experience just after we had finished writing our junior NECO examinations. Our class decided to have a mini-Olympic. We called it the 'STAC 9-Olympics'. In case you are wondering how we got the word 'STAC', we created it from the first letters of each class title. One of the highlights of the contest was something we called the 'Yabbing competition'. 'Yabbing' is vernacular for insulting. As funny as it sounds, the class nominated a classmate and me to go against a guy in another class.

We considered the young man the best 'insulter'. When the contest kicked off, he came up with his first lines. Everyone was thrilled; the best in this unworthy art was at it again. Then, I took a deep breath and, like a well-rehearsed speech, dropped my response in refutation to what he had said. Just as I ended, the crowd started to cheer and shouted that the guy should give up as it was a lost battle for him. And that was it. The contest ended there but the young man was injured. He became so cold. We were high school kids just having fun, but there we were, making another person feel less of who he was because we could take it.

You might wonder why I am sharing this lesson. Is it one of my laurels? Oh no! As a matter of fact, it is nothing to be proud of. But the point is clear – that you feel you are strong enough to handle what could break others does not mean you can throw it at them. Because they are not like you. We should understand one thing – we are not all the same. We are created individually with different temperaments.

Some people will break down because you did not respond to their greetings, while some wouldn't care. We respond to situations in different ways, and a lot of factors influence our actions. Remember that some people are going through unspeakable situations, hence, we shouldn't use ourselves as the standard to judge others. What you will take lightly can cause another man's death, so be very careful.

You are meant to be a source of light through your attitude. So even if you can condone terrible things from people, be the light by not giving out negative behaviors. You never know who is watching you. One action can be all that will catapult you to your realm of greatness. Whomever you do good or evil to may be the key to your progress in the next phase of your life.

It is human nature to want to underrate people, particularly when they are not in flashy clothes and shoes like us. But avoid being that way. Many people have secured their places in destiny through people they would have never imagined will help them in life. From the security guard outside the school's compound to the janitors, the teaching staff, and your friends, treat everyone with respect and honor them.

Know that if the man at the gate is not there to open the gate for you, you won't have access to inside the school, and without the janitors to clear the surroundings, you won't have a conducive environment to study. Without the teachers too, you cannot learn anything, because they must teach you what you need to know. And then your mates, including the ones you don't acknowledge, are what make the school an interesting place for you. You cannot go through school alone so everyone matters! Interestingly, we will discuss people in a later chapter in this book because they are an integral part of your bar-raising journey.

Be humble!

Humility is one of the most silent elevators of man. It has taken many people to levels they do not qualify for, and many times, don't merit. God's stand on humility is clear – "He exalts the humble and humbles those who exalt themselves." Pride is like cancer. It eats into you deeply without your knowledge and then unexpectedly cuts you short.

Endeavor to always search your heart to ensure that there's no element of pride in you. Many have missed it in life because they were too proud to adhere to simple instructions. The 'know it all' attitude won't take you anywhere. If you knew it all, you wouldn't have gotten into high school. So be humble.

Pride kills! Humility sustains life. If as a student, you owe every success to yourself and your abilities without acknowledging God, watch it! There's pride in you somewhere. When you start feeling too big to allow your educators to correct you, you should check yourself. When you begin to feel better than others, search your heart, because pride is approaching. When you begin to think or say you are too superior to learn from others, then it is crystal clear that you are the definition of pride. I have always believed that anyone too big to learn will be too small to excel.

At a point in my high school years, pride began to creep into my heart. But I was privileged to have had people around me who checked my excesses before they got out of hand and brought me back to my 'default state.' Proud people never go far because God restrains them (James 4:6). You can't want to share God's glory with Him, and you expect Him to cheer you when He has said to humanity that He doesn't share His glory.

You are called forth to show His excellence and not share His excellence. You are called to radiate His glory and not share His glory. Humility is a stimulator of God's lifting.

God's word states in James 4:10 that

Humble yourselves in the sight of the Lord, and he shall lift you up.
— James 4:10

This verse shows us that without humility, you cannot be a candidate for God's lifting; you know how fatal that will be. For you to be lifted, you must first be humble. Humility is a gateway to the world of opportunities. It showcases you and takes you far above your adversaries. See the lives of most great men. Many of them are humble.

In life, many people go up and fall drastically because of pride. There were students in the school who had started with good grades but, with time, let pride get the best of them and became shadows of their former selves. Funny enough, they seemed to care less, and that is because pride had eaten deep into them. Pride makes you feel right even when you know that you are wrong. It lets you take regrettable decisions even when you have better alternatives.

I detest pride so much because it is a destroyer of destiny. Its ruining power is second to none. Humility is easier and better than arrogance, so be humble so that you can be elevated.

Attitude is 100%

I started this chapter by saying that a good attitude is an asset, and that's because attitude is everything. It can take you up to the limelight or bring you down to dust. In whatever you do, build a great character that will outlive you. Attitude can take you to royalty even when you don't qualify for it. Asides from God's plan to take Joseph from the prison to the palace, Joseph's attitude stood him out. The Bible made us understand that Potiphar admired his ways and made him the head of his household long before he was thrown into prison.

There is a reason why attitude, of all things, determines one's altitude. Not hard work or determination, consistency, or integrity. These qualities alone are not enough for an individual's growth. Why? Because they all constitute the building blocks of a good character, which is also a good attitude.

In a place where everyone is qualified, your attitude will help you stand out. I watched a short video some time ago. Three job seekers had come for a job interview, and a janitor mopping the floor. Two of the applicants were rude to the cleaner while the third was kind to her. You can tell the rest of the story.

Your attitude is everything. Build it to draw wins and not problems for yourself. May you always be celebrated because of your attitude.

CHAPTER 5

o · · · · · · · · o

"BE SEPARATE"; KNOWLEDGE, TALENT, AND SKILLS MAKE YOU STAND OUT!

"Empowering means helping teams develop their skills and knowledge and spring them to use their talents."
– Ken Blanchard

One thing I've always known about knowledge, talent, and skills, is that they have the unique ability to make you stand out at any time and in any place. You know what you know, and you're in charge of it. Any skill you learn becomes yours, and when used properly, the sky becomes nothing more than a starting point. This trifecta's primary aim in your life is to always set you apart from the rest.

In the corporate world, what you have to offer often determines how far you will go. In high school, the same is true. Life is only as good as you make it, and how good you make it is entirely dependent on how well you use the knowledge, talents, and skills you've accumulated over time.

Friend, we live in the twenty-first century, and everyone wants their names in light and their faces on billboards, which is phenomenal. However, if you lack knowledge or squander your talents and skills, you might as well forget about those ambitions.

I once heard someone say "I want to die used and empty, with nothing else to give". I was amazed at what I thought at the time, was a HORRIBLE statement. As I pondered on it, I then realized that there is a lesson to learn from it. Believe me when I say that it has been my mantra since that day. "I must die empty!" Many people die without ever realizing their full potential. They die with a lot of unfinished business: mouths to feed, victories to win, and heights to reach. As a result, when a person has lived a fulfilled life, they have essentially died empty, because they have given the world everything

"BE SEPARATE"; KNOWLEDGE, TALENT, AND SKILLS MAKE YOU STAND OUT!

RAISING THE BAR AS A HIGH SCHOOL STUDENT

they have to offer.

You may not believe that your brain and skills are sufficient to help you achieve the potential that you know you possess. I've felt this way before, but if you can keep these three pillars in mind, you'll be well on your way to realizing your full potential.

You have it in you

One truth that has always existed and will always exist is that every human being possesses potential that, when used positively, can shape the world. We are expected to reach our full potential as human beings. Many of today's great individuals did not achieve success simply because they had the potential to do so. They were aware of their talent and skill, and instead of resting on their laurels, they pushed themselves even harder to reach their full potential. To put it another way, we are all destined for greatness. You, like Bezos and Musk, can make your dreams a reality. As a result, there's no difference between you and varsity football captain 'Tim Crawley,' who takes AP classes and has a 4.8 GPA, or popular cheerleader 'Nicole Vasquez,' who aces all her tests and debate tournaments. You may believe they have an advantage over you, but keep in mind that they have discovered their potential. Accordingly, the day you discover that thing you're naturally good at, you'll be taking the first step toward realizing your full potential. Try new things, participate in extracurricular activities, join clubs, or volunteer– you never know where you just might find yourself.

Isn't it fascinating how some people can reach deep into their minds and come up with ingenious ideas? Have you ever considered what is preventing you from doing the same, or how you can use the power of your mind to your advantage? The explanation isn't too far-fetched. Begin a journey of self-discovery, and you will be surprised at how fortunate you are; that you too are capable of greatness.

"Non Nobis Solum Nati Sumus (Not for Ourselves Alone Are We Born)"

- Marcus Tullius Cicero, 44 B.C

When you discover your gifts and hone them, they become yours for life. If you do not showcase these gifts to the world, however, they will die with you. Our gifts and talents are ours, but they do not belong solely to us. They are given to us for us to share them with others. Consider the world if no one

"BE SEPARATE"; KNOWLEDGE, TALENT, AND SKILLS MAKE YOU STAND OUT!

RAISING THE BAR AS A HIGH SCHOOL STUDENT

shared a talent. How depressing it would be! If Faraday kept his brilliant ideas to himself, or Lincoln never shared his knowledge and beliefs. Well, let's just say you won't even be reading this book.

Do not be the person who claims to have had the same idea as Zuckerberg, when YOU could have been Zuckerberg! Challenge yourself today. Break free from your comfort zone and join that club you've always wanted to join. High school clubs are fantastic places to discover your talents. Take charge of this stage of your life instead of remaining passive! You will become a force to be reckoned with the moment you begin doing so.

"If you've got an idea, start today. There's no better time than now to get going. That doesn't mean quit your job and jump into your idea 100% from day one, but there's always small progress that can be made to start the movement."
– Kevin Systrom, Instagram

Many years ago, the majority of high school students had no idea what an entrepreneur was, let alone that they could major in entrepreneurship in college. In 2019, however, the subject had piqued the interest of Gen Z, as almost half the students in middle and high school intended to start their own businesses. As a result of this growth, opportunities for entrepreneurship education in American schools have expanded significantly. According to research, as of 2015, 42 of the 50 states in the United States had K-12 guidelines or proficiency in entrepreneurial education. This number has since increased to 49 states, excluding Arizona, which reported entrepreneurship as a topic offered in a required course for graduation. In essence, all of these states must now include entrepreneurship education in their Career and Technical Education (CTE) pathways – all because of YOU. If you are a High schooler in the United States, you now have the opportunity to learn how to start a business.

As a teenager or young adult, regardless of your nationality, you have the advantage of TIME. This just means the earlier you begin, the more opportunities you will have to make mistakes and correct them.

Who said high school students couldn't be entrepreneurs? While in high school, I started a few businesses. I've always been business savvy if you will, and I told myself that I had to be a successful business leader. I started, and I'm still holding entrepreneurial sessions to get more young people on board with wealth creation. Begin right away and utilize your knowledge, talents, and skills. Holding them back will lead you nowhere.

"BE SEPARATE"; KNOWLEDGE, TALENT, AND SKILLS MAKE YOU STAND OUT!

RAISING THE BAR AS A HIGH SCHOOL STUDENT

In your lifetime, you have the opportunity to solve at least one problem. Don't deny the rest of the world the solution to that problem. Today, use that thing within you to offer a solution and be the difference.

Invest in yourself

When we start investing in ourselves, we become an asset. Being an asset as a person means that you are simply too valuable to the world to be replaced. Consider a man who gets everything he wants and finds everything he looks for. That man is not a demigod with supernatural abilities; he is simply an investor–a self-investor, to be precise. When an opportunity presents itself to a self-investor, do not regard it as luck or favoritism, but rather as a reward for taking steps toward his personal development.

Focusing on your personal development will help you understand yourself better as well as provide you with new skills and knowledge. You will gain a better understanding of your unique set of strengths, values, and passions, which you can then use to position yourself for golden opportunities when they present themselves.

When you have more than enough to offer everyone around you, you won't need to seek popularity or status. Believe me, it will all come to you. Imagine taking acting classes over the summer to improve your acting skills. When the summer is over and you begin a new year, the investment you made in yourself over the summer has prepared you to play a major role in any upcoming plays that year.

I firmly believe that what we do not try to understand as we grow, we will eventually stand under. The importance of knowledge in decorating one's life cannot be overstated because knowledge is light itself. The most well-known way to invest in yourself is to pursue a never-ending quest for knowledge and skills. Your talent, after all, is God-given, but as John C. Maxwell once said, "Talent is never enough." To become a complete person, you must hone your talents with knowledge and complement them with skills. This trio will elevate your career to new heights.

We are kings of what we know and slaves to what we do not, and many pay dearly for the latter. A person's elevator is knowledge. It has the potential to propel you to heights you never thought possible. It is power.

When you combine your knowledge with your skills, you will be miles ahead of your contemporaries. To improve yourself, one must constantly

49

"BE SEPARATE"; KNOWLEDGE, TALENT, AND SKILLS MAKE YOU STAND OUT!

RAISING THE BAR AS A HIGH SCHOOL STUDENT

seek knowledge and learn how to apply it. You are not a knowledge island, so strive to know more and empower your mind.

Scientists concluded that a man uses only about four percent of his brain in his lifetime and that Albert Einstein was the only person who pushed his brain a little more. I then asked myself, "What would I become if I used just about ten percent of my brain?" A Supercomputer? A machine? A robot? What are your thoughts? I am quite confident that I will outperform all three because it has been scientifically proven that humans are smarter than computers.

When you pursue knowledge, success follows. When you lack knowledge, stop chasing success. If you pursue knowledge, success will follow. I am addicted to success, so I constantly invest in myself by reading books, attending training programs, and taking courses.

Everything good is the result of the application of knowledge and skills. The knowledge you have will help you learn new skills. Thus, knowledge and skills work in tandem, and without application, neither is useful. This is where many people get it wrong: they continue to feed their intellect with every resource they come across while applying none of the insights gained. If you fall into this category, you should stop wasting your time. It is simply futile, like working for money you cannot spend.

It will benefit you as a student to always seek knowledge and apply what you know. In doing so, never underestimate anyone or feel too big to learn from others, because believing you know it all is a first-class ticket to failure. Many people have been led astray by the know-it-all mentality.

As a high schooler, I never hesitated to study with friends or meet with teachers for help, and the effects were evident in my grades. I often thought of it as collaborative learning. No one in our study group can claim that collaborative learning did not help them achieve academic success. –Friend, I think you should also try learning with other friends–. Finland has the best educational system in the world, and collaborative learning is one of the secrets to its success.

Learning with others is one of the best ways to learn, and learning from those with experience is the best way to avoid regrettable mistakes.

It is imperative that you understand that not everything you come across is for your consumption. As some foods are considered unhealthy, there are some philosophies and skills that should not be consumed. Be cautious of

"BE SEPARATE"; KNOWLEDGE, TALENT, AND SKILLS MAKE YOU STAND OUT!

RAISING THE BAR AS A HIGH SCHOOL STUDENT

such. You are still young, and you should not overindulge yourself. Feed only what you require, and what you require is always appropriate. Don't be duped into getting what you want or being influenced to want what you know is not right for you.

Knowledge and skills are valuable, but when obtained from the wrong sources, they really start to stink. Oh, there is nothing more malodorous than hearing a person speak out utter ignorance. You don't want anything to destroy you, so filter what you learn. We are allowed to be sensitive in our pursuit of knowledge and skills. After all, we are not robots programmed to absorb every piece of information that comes our way.

Treasure your opportunities

The bridge at which the trio of 'knowledge, talents, and skills' meet 'excellence' is 'opportunities'. Opportunity links your knowledge, talents, or skill with excellence. Every good opportunity is a shot at success. I've had experiences that others did not have simply because I made myself available when opportunities arose. The strange thing about opportunities is that they do not seek you out. You should search for them. It doesn't knock, rather, "it presents itself when you beat down the door," as Kyle Chandler once said.

Some people just can't seem to get it right because they have repeatedly dropped the ball on certain opportunities. Every opportunity, you see, is a platform for revealing the things buried within you. Don't joke with opportunities so that you don't joke with your future. It is important to note that for you to make a profit from any opportunity, you must go through a three-fold process I call 'The SSU-Process' – Search, Scrutinize and Utilize.

- **Search** – I previously stated that opportunities do not seek anyone, but rather that people seek opportunities. The twenty-first century is full of diverse opportunities, and these opportunities are available to anyone who wants them.
  Back in high school, I was always looking for ways to improve myself. As a result, there was no competition that I was unaware of. Despite choosing a STEM pathway in high school, I represented the school in a number of debate tournaments and championships, directed a number of plays, and acted in a few of them. Simultaneously, I played saxophone in the orchestra and sang in the choir – remember, with "a STEM pathway." If all men are given equal opportunities, then every man has the potential to succeed. Friend, you have been given a golden opportunity, which is the education you are currently

"BE SEPARATE"; KNOWLEDGE, TALENT, AND SKILLS MAKE YOU STAND OUT!

RAISING THE BAR AS A HIGH SCHOOL STUDENT

receiving. It is now your responsibility to provide yourself with more opportunities. "If opportunity doesn't knock, build a door," said Milton Berle

I once attended the Future Africa Ambassadors Twelve-week forum, which is a seminar series in which African development experts share their views on the continent's growth trajectory. Deepshikha Parmessur, Prime Minister of the Mauritius National Youth Parliament, spoke at one of the sessions, and she spoke THE TRUTH. Her words stuck with me: "If there is no seat at the table, make your own table or better still, bring your own seat."

We complain a lot about how the government, our parents, school policies, and other factors are to blame for our inability to succeed, but we rarely take the time to reflect. Do you still believe this? Because the days of teenagers having the entire world at their fingertips are long gone. When parents provided for all our needs and WANT, and school districts ensured we had EVERYTHING we needed to succeed. We cannot even rely on our governments anymore! Many teenagers and young adults around the world lack access to basic resources such as electricity, a good education, and so on.

So, when we really NEED something TODAY, we have got to GO OUT and GET IT OURSELVES.

It is in your pursuit of opportunities that you will find the ones that will catapult you into greatness.

- **Scrutinize** –During the COVID-19 pandemic, I signed up for an online tournament that promised an $800 prize to the winner. I took advantage of the offer and paid a $3 registration fee – I never entered that tournament–. In fact, it never existed in the first place. C'est la vie, I suppose. I accepted the loss and took responsibility for my mistake, despite how painful it was to know that someone out there played on my intelligence or lack thereof.

One quote that has become all too familiar to me is, "Never mistake opportunities for fate because THAT can be fatal." When an opportunity seems too good to be true, it most likely is. All you have to do is keep your wits about you. Some opportunities are ploys to make you look foolish, so, be smart — don't fall for them. It is critical for you to avoid getting overly excited about opportunities that

"BE SEPARATE"; KNOWLEDGE, TALENT, AND SKILLS MAKE YOU STAND OUT!

RAISING THE BAR AS A HIGH SCHOOL STUDENT

appear to be unbelievably beneficial to your advancement. When I first started making money online, I was aware of two things; my golden rules, if you will. That is, any platform that requests referrals or promises a high ROI in exchange for a small investment was suspicious. There are very few platforms in the world that can deliver on that promise, and the "Make Money Online" Ad you came across on that insecure website lacking an SSL certificate is most emphatically not one of them.

The place of scrutiny when pursuing opportunities should never be underestimated. Many people waste time engaging in activities that end up causing them pain. Being able to discern is one of our most powerful abilities as humans. So, before you enter any seemingly advantageous situation, thoroughly investigate it. Examine it twice to ensure that it is worthwhile.

Anything that appears to be too good to be true should be approached with caution or avoided entirely. It is painful, however, that some of the best opportunities often disappoint. As a result, before we jump at any opportunities, we should scrutinize and be certain that they will not leave us in disarray later.

Examining opportunities will keep you out of trouble, and you can never be too cautious when it comes to avoiding problems.

- **Utilize** – At the end of the day, the purpose of any opportunity is determined by how it is utilized. As a high school student, you set yourself apart from your peers by seizing opportunities. Following caution and scrutinization, it is up to you to ensure that you don't let it slip.

Never pass up a good opportunity. You have one right now – the luxury of high-quality education. . If you use it wisely, you will instantly become a potential solution to any problem that exists. However, if you choose to do otherwise, you become a liability to both yourself and society. Your parents are already putting in a lot of effort to see you through high school, so how do you intend to repay them?

When I saw how hard my mother worked to ensure that I finished school, I didn't need anyone to tell me that I should appreciate the opportunity that had been given to me. I valued every aspect of it and

"BE SEPARATE"; KNOWLEDGE, TALENT, AND SKILLS MAKE YOU STAND OUT!

RAISING THE BAR AS A HIGH SCHOOL STUDENT

gave it my all. You're reading this today because I had a fantastic experience that I'd like to share with you. In any other case, you would not be able to hold a copy of this book.

Another opportunity you now have is to put into practice everything you have learned from this book and any other book you will or have ever read. It is a chance for you to learn, unlearn, and relearn. No one wants regret, but to avoid one, you should take advantage of previously evaluated opportunities and channel them into making your life better.

Remember, we are always striving to be better versions of ourselves. Opportunities will assist you in achieving this natural goal.

It is not the opportunity you have that promotes you, but the one you take advantage of. A personal relationship with the CEO of a multinational does not guarantee you a good job. However, it is when you decide to leverage that personal relationship with said CEO, that you have a chance at getting that job. Similarly, as a student, it is not enough to be aware of all the championships happening during the school year; you must participate in at least one of them.

Apply what you know

The difference between knowledge and wisdom is quite simple. Knowledge is what you know but wisdom is putting into practice what you know. The practical application of knowledge is what categorizes you as a wise person. What you know stays in your head but when you put what you know into practice, it stands you out. The reason most people lose is not that they don't know how to go about it, but they have chosen to be the "knowers", but never the "doers".

It is insanity to know what to do and not do it. Consider an AP English student who learns new words at the start of the week but does not use them in his writing, instead, relying on basic grammar and vocabulary. What do you think will happen to him? The issue here is not that he didn't know what to do, but that he didn't think hard enough to figure out how to apply his advanced vocabulary knowledge to his work in order to pass.

If you think about it, what is the point of knowledge if it cannot be applied? You are not a storage device. You are a smart young man or woman who is expected to be transformed, renewed, and rejuvenated by the

"BE SEPARATE"; KNOWLEDGE, TALENT, AND SKILLS MAKE YOU STAND OUT!

RAISING THE BAR AS A HIGH SCHOOL STUDENT

knowledge you possess.

The logic of 'practical application' extends to our talents and skills. No one will know you have a beautiful voice unless you pick up the mic and sing. No one will know you are a computer guru unless you pick up a computer and demonstrate your abilities.

I once promised myself that if I was not going to use any knowledge or skill, there was no point in acquiring it because my head needed space to store only things I would use. This is why I don't go to every conference or training. I also don't listen to the words of every great speaker, with the exception of a few. I don't enroll in every class, especially now that every young person is enrolled in every programming class.

In the world of technology, there is a phenomenon known as information overload. When a system has more information than it requires. Now, the emphasis is on the word 'needs,' because you do not need everything; you only need what you will use, so stop wasting time. Understand your path and engage with what keeps you on it. That is the best way to determine whether you need to learn a new skill or attend a class. Avoid participating in some of these activities simply because your close friends are doing so. Friend, just as your fingerprints are unique, so is your destiny.

Once you can discern what your path is, it will help you make the best of your time while in high school and even as you journey through life, because you will make use of your knowledge, talents, and skills.

You are light!

The illuminating power of light can never be denied. The light is within you, and it is your responsibility to illuminate the earth. The world is becoming too dark, and it requires your profound light. Allow the world to see your talent, skill, or knowledge. Don't hide it any longer. Allow your friends and teachers to see it, as well as your family.

As I frequently say, we all have the keys to solving a specific problem in the world. The key is that little guy buried inside of you who is trying to break free. Don't hold it down any longer.

There is no better time than now to let it out.

Enough of complaining about the world's problems. Make use of your

"BE SEPARATE"; KNOWLEDGE, TALENT, AND SKILLS MAKE YOU STAND OUT!

RAISING THE BAR AS A HIGH SCHOOL STUDENT

skills to solve them. Because you are light, use what you know to deal with them and leverage your skills to overcome them. I'm looking forward to hearing about you, and the great solution you came up with.

CHAPTER 6

o · · · · · · · · o

YOUR COMPANY DETERMINES
WHAT ACCOMPANIES YOU

"Bad company corrupts good character."
– Menander

Writing this chapter makes me feel extremely emotional because as I write each word, my mind flashes back to the great people I have encountered throughout my short time on this planet.

I feel fortunate to be surrounded by some of the most amazing people in the world. I would gladly say that the support I receive from my network, starting with my family, has been really fantastic. And without the assistance of these so many wonderful people, I would not be where I am today. In fact, I would not have finished High School without the help of the good people who had invested in my success.

In the undying words of 17th Century English author, John Donne: "No one is self-sufficient; an island, entire of itself". You have probably heard before that you will need people to get through in life. You cannot do it by yourself– no one can. It is demanding and requires you to go through it with others. Donne continued, saying; "every man is a piece of the continent, a part of the main". In this chapter, I commenced my address by thanking my "network." Why? As the English Author implied, "no human being exists in isolation." We are, as Aristotle pointed out, "Social Animals" by nature, and cannot "live alone".

The words of John Donne made it clear that we all exist in a network, and as you and I both know, a network exists because of a connection between a series of individual entities. As a result, he believes that we are all "pieces of the continent." We require the next person just as much as they require us. If you enjoy The Walking Dead as I do, you are probably familiar with the character "Negan" and his belief that "people are a resource." As much as any TWD fan would hate to admit it, he was correct.

The greatest gift we all possess as human beings on this planet is our fellow human beings—A person to care for us; a person whom we are to care for, and a person to assist us in times of need.

Therefore, does this, however, imply that all human beings are good; kind enough to tolerate their fellow human beings? Certainly not. You will meet both the mean and the kind in High School, but one thing that you must know is that everyone comes into your life for a reason. You have come this far in reading this book because I also have a role to play in your life. As a result, we all have a role to play in the lives of those whom we come across throughout our daily activities.

Now, it is up to you to decide on what to do, and what the best way to go about it is? Setting certain goals for yourself, and making a decision on how to actualize them leads you to your God-ordained company when you can answer the question of what you do and how you do it in the lives of others. It is important to remember, also, that the first company you will naturally find yourself in will be your family.

The family is the cradle of socialization, and how you interact with others in that substantial group predicts how you will interact with others, particularly in the outside world.

My words of affirmation while in High School were: "I will be committed to helping others because that is one way I can be raised", and these did work out perfectly. I spent a lot of time with the people I met in High School, mentoring some; assisting others academically, and motivating so many. The beauty of this is that I reaped a lot for every seed I planted in each of them!

Also, I would say the issue is not meeting people, but rather, meeting the right set of people because it is easier to become exactly what those around you are. Now, let us take a look at some of the people in your life right now who are fundamental, particularly to your success in high school.

- **Family** – Your family is the first set of people you come across in life, especially your nuclear family. The kind of relationship you have with them determines how well you will relate with others in society. My nuclear family consists of my mother, brother, and me; it is always a pleasure being in their company. We quarrel and make-up, we enjoy and endure, cry and laugh; in all, we have an unbreakable bond.

In the same vein, my family is my primary source of strength. Can you say the same for yours? Now, when the going is not good, your family should be your first point of call because they are the ones that keep cheering you on the most till you get to the finish line. So, do not take them for granted.

How do you treat your parents; do you handle them with great care? The last time I checked, they are the initiators of your family and so, you must accord them the utmost respect. Parents symbolize the first earthly representative of every child. Therefore, permit me to say that even if your parents are not on the right path, it is not in your place to judge them. Doing so means you disregard their superiority over you. Leave their imperfections to be corrected by their peers; or better still, those whom they look up to.

A very good way to secure success even beyond High School is through a formidable family relationship. And always remember that your family's importance plays a great key role in your academic excellence.

Now, let's discuss siblings. Siblings; are the gifts that you cannot live without when you are given, and that you might not even be bothered by if you are not given. My brother is the best support I could ask for. There are times when we argue; yell at each other, and so on. On good days, these occurrences merely become history. I can remember, my brother was the last person to call me that night when I first arrived in New York, and we kept saying our goodbyes over the phone for hours. As absurd as it may sound, neither of us wanted the call to end. The bond of family is unmatched by anything, in that sense.

Discussing other relatives. There are grand mysteries behind why the family included the extended family in addition to the nuclear family. I will explain why: Your nuclear family may not always have the resources to help you out when you are in desperate need of it. However, you could still receive assistance from within by way of your other family rather than going outside in search of assistance. Therefore, show them the same kind of affection you give your primary family because you never know the day you will need them the most.

59

When everything goes to hell, the people who stand by you without flinching – they are your family. - **Jim Butcher**

How Profound! Make it a point of responsibility to make sure that love, peace, and harmony flourish in your home because a content family is essential for you to raise your bars. You might seem little, but you are just as crucial as the decision-makers. To accomplish this, you must be careful to avoid raising any issues in your home. When things go well for your family, it opens the way for your own success.

- **Friends** - I've always felt that we might find friends who end up being like family to us, but you must first realize that friendship is not something that is forced upon you; rather, it is something that you choose to have. Because support should be a key requirement for friendship, I have been able to gradually develop a large network of resourceful friends who support my goals. What are you two doing together if not supporting one another?

While support is essential, many would add that trust is equally very important to keep a good friendship. In one of Dhar Mann's videos, one of the actors said to his friend that "If they don't have trust, then they don't have anything." Very simple to say, yet challenging to put into practice.

However, given the unpredictable nature of people, the question of trust in friendships is a highly risky one. I, therefore, subscribe to the school of thought that says you should love everyone but use caution when putting your trust in anyone to prevent unfavorable occurrences. Speaking of unwelcome events, this is the reason why High School students are typically advised to avoid being in relationships that may involve a great deal of commitment since their minds are too delicate to handle situations like break-ups when they occur. That is not to imply that you should not be loyal to your friends, but as was previously stated, "be cautioned."

I am a tenacious advocate of wisdom application in every relationship I discover myself, because anything that involves two or more humans is inevitably bound to have little challenges. Nevertheless, when wisdom is at work, it is easier for things to fall in place notwithstanding the initial circumstances. For instance, wisdom will dictate to you how you would respond if a close friend offends you with hurtful comments after being provoked.

Every good friend is positioned in your life to lift you. It is not a good idea to spend time with people that are not in line with the pursuit of your purpose. Once, I asked a dear friend "What about your other friends? I realize you don't speak very often about them." I was amazed by her response. She confided in me that she was yet to find other friends to encourage her in achieving her goals in life.

It has been said that bad communication, or even worse, bad friends, are the primary corruptors of decent manners. The wrong friends become like clogs in the wheel of the fulfillment of your destiny. I am not sure you would like there to be any hindrance in your pursuit to make history by fulfilling your destiny.

Friendship thrives better when it is mutually beneficial to the parties involved.

The best kind of (biological) interaction is called Symbiosis. It's "Symbiosis", because each creature gains from it, according to Biology. I want you to ask yourself this two-sided question about all your close friends: "What am I benefiting from this person, and what is he benefiting from me?" You can decide to list all their names out and do this one after the other.

There is an issue if there is somebody from whom you are not receiving any positive benefits, and vice versa if they are not receiving any positive benefits from you. That's how easy it is. Choose your friends carefully since friendship is about adding value.

Teachers – "Being good is noble, but teaching others to be good is nobler and less troublesome", as Mark Twain famously observed. Any person's growth and development are greatly influenced by teachers. In High School, I got along well with a few teachers, and our friendship birthed some amazing achievements.

If you think about it logically, you spend an average of 45 hours per week in class with your teachers throughout the nine months you are in school each year. This implies that throughout nine months, you will spend more than a third of each day with your teachers. This incredibly demonstrates the importance of instructors in our life.

It is quite disappointing that teachers don't get paid enough for their work. I was moved while reading about outstanding teachers in my mentor Dele Aina's book 'Chalk Power'. To understand how crucial teachers are in shaping lives, you should read the book. It was educational to read the various accounts of how students benefited from teachers in one way or another.

Being at odds with your teachers, or even worse, not understanding, and disregarding them are the worst mistakes you may make in High School.

If I was successful in High School, it was likely due to the many teachers who gave me the motivation to persevere. In October 2019, I had a thought-provoking conversation with Mr. Taiwo Adenariwo. He was the Vice-Principal (academics) of my school and was responsible for driving me to school nearly every day. This conversation gave me a newfound zest for life. Ever heard me talk about defining yourself? The conversation that morning shed light on my existence. I might not be where I am now if I had a bad relationship with him.

Interestingly, I still get along well with some of my teachers. In actuality, my relationship with these "some" has changed from being one of teacher and pupil to one of friend and family. There is no way you could read my story and miss the impacts of Mrs. Olubanke Ohunenese or Mrs. Odunayo Akinboboye, and Mrs. Doris Dozie— these are the people who, from the start, have always had my best interests at heart and have inspired me to keep improving.

Whenever I'm exhausted, I run to them, and they encourage me to finish the race. They constantly remind me how much they are rooting for me and praying for me. They were there to check my excesses and rectify them. They are great people.

Your teachers act as if they had been your parents. Building a strong relationship with your teachers will be easier if you start to think of them as your parents. Never let your guard down and stop considering the advice of your teachers. It would be a very costly mistake that will cause you to go downhill.

- **Mentors** – I consider myself fortunate to have realized the value of mentorship at a very tender age. This assisted in redefining myself and setting me on the proper course of my life. The adage goes: "Experience is the best teacher". It is just as beneficial to learn from someone else's experience as it is to actually have the experience yourself. Would you like to test the temperature of the fire with a finger dipped in it? Or would you rather hear from someone else who has had the experience and can explain it to you?

In the first chapter, I wrote about getting prepared for the journey of High School. Having people who have gone before you share their experiences with you on the ups and downs they encountered is one of the finest methods to prepare. Mentorship is the result of this process. It entails asking for advice from someone who is more experienced than you in a particular area of life.

Mentors help to sharpen you in line with your destiny. They have walked the road you are trying to go through and they know the nitty-gritty of what the journey entails. I had several mentors in High School; students, teachers, and others from outside. This translated me into a man with different people replicated in him. For instance, I love leadership so much, therefore I searched for an expert in that area.

As a result, I discovered a monarch in that sector in my mentor, Sylvester Jenkins, who not only provides me with incredible assistance but is also one of many fathers I look up to.

In the aspect of life and personal development, Dele Aina has graduated from being just my mentor but now a fatherly figure and it has been a most enjoyable journey growing up under his tutelage. His commitment to developing great people caught my attention and I decided to run with a similar commitment. You need someone to align you with your purpose and to keep you constantly in the pursuit of your purpose. Mentors help to give you a direction that heads you to your destination.

When you have a mentor, you have someone that will provide you with guidance, motivation, and initiative that will keep you on the pathway to greatness. A man without a mentor is like a sheep without a shepherd. Therefore, you need to find someone that will root for you every time. Someone who has positive intentions to grow you into a total individual.

However, selecting a mentor could be challenging because there are those "wolves in sheep's clothing" whose life goal is to harm while disguising as assistance. So, when looking for a mentor, try to follow the proper storyline and achievements of those in that field. Be aware that most people prefer to mentor those with whom they already have a personal bond.

Thus, I strongly recommend that you grow a relationship first with anyone you wish to have as a mentor before requesting mentorship. Moreso, mentoring someone who already has something in hand is preferable to mentoring someone who has not yet started. This is so that the degree of intentionality might vary. In light of this, it is essential that you first create a niche for yourself and begin to expand it before asking someone to mentor you. The concept of mentoring is similar to getting a head start on your goals. In essence, you receive assistance from someone to get you to your objective rather than doing it yourself.

- **Role Models** – As children, each of us had a childhood role model who we admired from a distance and aspired to be like. Some of us developed an obsession with these models, and we began attempting to act, walk, talk, and even dress like them. The funny thing is, sometimes we never get to meet these people in person throughout our lives, but we already have a strong desire to emulate them. For this reason, they are known as "Role Models".

You already know how important a role model is, so I won't even start there. Instead, "Who is your role model, though?", is the viewpoint I'll take. While role models are critical to making the most of your time in High School and generally in life. It is crucial to understand that the model you choose to follow will determine how far in life you travel North or South.

If you decide to emulate hooligans, it will be of no surprise when you eventually turn out to be one. But should you decide to do otherwise, the expectations that you have for yourself will become evident. John C. Maxwell's eloquence and adept knowledge of leadership attracted him to me. When I was contesting for the Senior Prefect role in High School, one of his quotes on leadership was my starting line. Thus, I have seen myself transformed to become like him or even better from a young age. I dare say that I could be the John C. Maxwell of my generation.

In the year 2020 alone, I had more than thirty speaking engagements. Many were for international events, while others were for Nigerian local events. Therefore, no one should be surprised by my stride as it is how my role models live. That is how influential role models can be, especially if you internalize their excellent traits. If you choose a role model for yourself that has no positive impact on the world, you are destined to hinder your personal growth. I believe you ought to know where you want to go at this point in your life.

Consequently, you should choose someone whose life will serve as a guide to you from afar. Role Models seem very insignificant but they are important. Left to me, I would say it all depends on how open you are to taking lessons from their lives and using them to help you in your journey.

A role model doesn't necessarily have to be that famous person you see on the screen or Instagram every day. It is always exciting when I hear some people state confidently that either of their parents is their role model. Your role model can be that senior in your school or a relative or a teacher. Do not forget that you are limitless in choosing role models because again, everyone has a purpose in your life so do not tie yourself down to that guy on Instagram. Explore and pick different people whose lives serve as learning aids to you.

The Greatest Role Model - Christ

While you allow Christ to triumph over your life, let me start by saying that the relationship you have also with your dreams and career, serves as the beginning of every other thing for you. No man neglects Christ and lives a triumphant life. The fact that you exist is not based on your IQ, at all, but rather, to thrive exceptionally well on earth and be free from all oppression. We will further this relationship with role models extensively in the later chapter of this book. But till then, let us look at the "Greatest Role Model".

One of the best gifts that existence offers us as human beings is the empowerment to live after the order of Christ. Interestingly, that's the whole essence of Creation – To live an impactful life. A life that is categorized as worth living. As fate would have it, all we need to do is to pick the lifestyle for every situation and stick to it. To me, it is a walk that has been made easy as a result of the existence of creation, and we have the best eidolon to look up to.

There have been great people who came into the earth and left footprints of remembrance. They came and showed us how to cultivate the attitude of "bar-raising". They raised many bars during their lifetime on earth. You have everything within your reach (parents, friends, teachers, mentors, and role models). Therefore, your relationship with Christ, and your dreams are the perfect example to follow. They are the 'Model of models' so, you are good when you look up to them.

Role Models— again, they are the best model and leaders you can look up to and mold your life after because in them lies perfection. To live after the order of Christ-like pathways, and your dreams, you must be empowered to do so. If you look closely at the life of every role model that surrounds you, you will discover that there were lots of steps they took that the average human will find hard to take but took them and raised insurmountable bars with them. You could also raise insurmountable bars in life by putting in a serious commitment.

Nothing stands you out more than living the way you dream to live. Benjamin Carson's book, 'You Have A Brain', reminds us of an amazing narrative that simply inspires and motivates you to give your best in life! No matter where you come from or your background, anyone can succeed if they give their best.

I was introduced to this book by a junior High School teacher who was planning to use it in her classes. Supposedly it was about a successful pediatric neurosurgeon giving accolades to people who helped him develop himself. That attracted me since I also feel such intense gratitude for so many; some that I am aware of, and some that I never realized were there. I will say he delivers that, and also provides some very good ideas about how to get on track and stay on track for "success". I rated the book higher. Not to overstate that, though, and I have recommended the book to several people— especially to parents of preteens, and college students who might be inspired by his storyline. It is a fairly well-written book, and easy to read.

I once spoke to a mother figure in my life and she outrightly declared that the only best way to have our dreams come true is to emulate an established role model. The greatest role model on earth is one that demonstrates the epitome of every good virtue that exists. Think about it, if everyone on earth pursued their dreams, and gave it their very best, perhaps the world would be a thousand times better than it is now. Role Model figures are so simple

YOUR COMPANY DETERMINES WHAT ACCOMPANIES YOU

RAISING THE BAR AS A HIGH SCHOOL STUDENT

and easy to live after. The question, therefore, is have you made up your mind to take every step they took and speak every word they declared and do everything they sacrificed while on earth? Of course, I do not mean you are dying for the world because that is not your divine assignment on earth. So, do not let your mind begin to pace about now.

As human beings, that standard of living has been architectured for everyone on earth to follow notwithstanding their social strata. Ever since I got my mind made up not to look backward, it has been a pleasurable experience. I have the potential laid down in my heart to guide me in my journey on earth. I remember once on the 10th of January, 2022; I was in the bathroom preparing to shower and a word dropped in my heart while I was lost in thought: "The day you begin to feel that you have arrived, I will bring you back to where you are coming from." What? I was so astonished. Encounters like that imply the essence of consciously and passionately desiring to embrace the "Greatest Role Model".

Whose Fault Is It?

Many individuals tend to blame others for their failures or losses, but I want you to change such a mentality right away. Your destiny is in your hands to run according to how your life has been designed, thus you must learn to accept accountability for yourself and your actions. Therefore, the person luring you into doing something that violates your moral principles is not the issue. Instead, you are the issue, my friend. You are the one who has decided to continue with someone who is determined to destroy you.

Stop apportioning blame to people for anything, especially things that are not working in your life. You can choose to associate yourself with illustrious individuals who will inspire you to make the most of your time in High School and your life in general. I always had this strong principle in High School – If there is a friend or acquaintance that is trying to take me off balance, then that is no good friend and instead of keeping along, I should do away with them.

You are the primary cause of any issue that arises in your life as a result of the company you keep. A friend once shared with me a narrative that her brother made friends with some bad guys and he is always trying to feign that he will never end up like them because to him, he's always cautious of things around him. Three weeks after she told me about her brother, the young man had begun to smoke. It saddens me that from the story, one confirms the essence of the familiar saying that "Bad companionship corrupts good

67

manners". So, the problem is not anyone, at all— instead, you!

"Always believe in yourself and always stretch yourself beyond your limits. Your life is worth a lot more than you think because you are capable of accomplishing more than you know. You have more potential than you think, but you will never know your full potential unless you keep challenging yourself and pushing beyond your own self-imposed limits." -
Roy T. Bennett

The year 2021 was a very interesting year for me particularly because of some unusual moves I made. I would go round the streets in my community, sharing inspiring handbooks with people, educating them on carrying out their goals, engaging in existential benefits, and so on. Did I get my paycheck? Oh! Yes, I did, and not only that; I profited greatly. The profit of my tireless walk really thus transformed me today from a local champion to a global figure.

Furthermore, consistency pays. Your dreams can never and will never be a problem because if you put your full best into it, and with commitment, they will come true, surely.

Also, is it your parents, perhaps? No decent parent worth their salt would want anything bad to happen to their child(ren). Therefore, identify your areas of error and start making amends. I am also aware that some kids are carelessly being born into the world without a clearer plan on how to care for them, and that some other kids may unluckily suffer from illness, lose their jobs, or in the worst-case situations, pass away. All of these peculiar occurrences are known to parental care.

However, as Bill Gates once stated, "It is not your fault if you are born poor but it is your fault if you die poor," whether or not you will succeed in High School is still in your control. The world is too wide a stage for you, my friend; play your part as best you can, then let your efforts reward you. Do not let anything stop you from achieving your goals since you will always be responsible for the outcome; be it positive or negative.

You will meet the right people

I have always thought that the responsibility of raising men could be done by humans. They most often take the form of family, close friends, co-workers, partners, elders, sisters, and brothers to ensure some support. You might be wondering where your ideal assistant or companion is, but I want to reassure you that they are out there and that they wouldn't stop working until they fulfill their destiny in your life. In every sphere of life, I have witnessed the development of great persons who will serve humanity. Abraham Lincoln was born and raised in an environment that looks too unfavorable for human habitation. And given the mission to transform American society, he performed twice as well as any previous incumbent, and his reign is still remembered.

We also remember the well-known tale of Thomas Edison, who struggled in High School and was turned away due to his poor academic performance, but who rose to fame later in life as the technology world's savior, using his inventions to save humanity. Your level of readiness to receive the proper person, so that your reception of him does not drive him away from accomplishing his mission in your life, is the only thing keeping him from coming to you. So, to draw the proper people to you, you must exercise patience and never stop working on yourself.

Furthermore, you must also keep making investments in yourself if you want to develop a life of comfort and possess valuable assets. Everyone prefers to invest in assets rather than liabilities because only assets are intended to produce significant returns. It is crucial to always believe in your potential, and not in humankind, too. The reason for this is that a guy's ability to assist another man is completely constrained.

While in High School and even till now, I have been blessed by different people that have been positioned to uplift me. Someone once asked me "How do you know all these people?" I laughed and said, "If you can do what I do, then you would know more." What then do I do? I constantly prepare myself while waiting for the helpers that have been raised to promote me. I also carry myself in such a way that when you help me, you will see it as you are equally doing yourself great good so, you do not act like you are doing me a favor but you are simply fulfilling destiny.

Now, there are certain people you think will be a big help to you, but finding out that they don't seem to have your best interests in mind can be pretty depressing. This should give you some solace: Nobody is indispensable. If he is unable to bless you, another person will be easily raised to do so. Additionally, keep in mind that no one has a permanent place in your life; hence, those who are pleasant today may become repulsive tomorrow. Keep your cool, give thanks for the good moments, and move on; excellent people will still arrive.

Also, when one party is constantly on the receiving end, this is one of the factors that makes a relationship poisonous; it can be extremely draining and frustrating. The greatest approach to prevent this is to always wish to give back or occasionally provide one or two items. An extremely useful illustration is if you have a friend or relative living with you at your home. How would you feel if you were the only one in the house doing all of the cooking, cleaning, and paying bills? No matter how tolerant you are, you would throw the guy out.

Due to this, you must make sure that your contributions; no matter how small they are, are made equally by everybody. It doesn't hurt to buy a box of chocolates for a friend who is always willing to assist you in understanding concepts in class or to write your teachers a short message of appreciation. It simply increases their desire to help you more. When I was still in charge of the Nigerian team at Youngazu, I once texted my coworkers to express my affection for them.

On that day, I received a lot of love in return, and many of them gave me additional assurances of their unwavering support for me to keep having an impact. Consider this: If I had told them to start working, I probably would have come across as the grumpy, mean boss, but on that particular day, everyone regarded me as a friend, and this had a significant impact on our overall impact statistics for 2021 because we reached out to over 750 people in 2021, which is triple the total number of people we had reached out to in 2020 since we began. So don't just take; give as well, for persistent giving is what makes it possible for you to get.

Make The Best Of Every Good Relationship

Every interaction, as we have established, either moves you upward or below. It is now up to you to effectively use all of your positive relationships to succeed in life. Every positive relationship is like a chance to bring out the best in you, but to be a candidate for this, you must make the most of the relationship. After all, as you are already aware, opportunities must be taken advantage of, to benefit from them.

Given this, it is one thing to be interested in a side hustle, like freelance writing. Herein, you can make a passive income to support yourself. It is now advantageous to have a young friend who is engaged in freelancing, but it is quite another to take advantage of your friendship with this friend to advance your understanding of this industry and launch your career. Can you see how it works? Many folks seriously miss it here. They abandon what will genuinely benefit them greatly in favor of chasing after what does not exist.

Before gazing outside. Therefore, do well to always check within, before gazing your way out. I cannot see reasonings in having a relationship with a person who is knowledgeable enough in a particular profession and yet, still keeps an eye out for them. You now know that anyone with whom you have a relationship, and who does not have your best interests at heart, is not someone you should roll with. So, do not suggest that some people don't enjoy assisting others. However, this is not a license to imply that, just because you know one individual, you should not expand your knowledge dealing with other sources, no! But instead, to progress, it is smarter to start small while you work your way up.

I have heard a lot of young people lament that certain people at the top do not want to help them out. Nobody should be left behind is a notion I support. In that case, when I stand, I ought to make sure that everyone in my circle stands as well. As a result, I have developed long-lasting relationships with several individuals from around the globe. When you both support each other when necessary, any relationship will be most enjoyable.

Let Them Go!

When someone's purpose in your life is fulfilled, one of the hardest things that happen is to let them go, especially if you have a strong link with them. It could not always be a problem that keeps you from that individual with whom you formerly had a wonderful relationship. Other elements could include a change in the environment, a change in one's standing, or even, very frequently, an abrupt and unanticipated cut-off. But after spending a lot of time together, your connection with that person may have become strained for a variety of reasons, including those listed above.

However, this is merely a sign that you both need to move on because their time in your life has come to an end. I once witnessed the choir of the Mormon Tabernacle bid Alex Boye farewell. Although it was a very emotional event, its sole purpose was to elevate both parties. Now, let us focus on the positive, for it is our major concern: sometimes you and I need to part ways to advance in life and learn more about ourselves. Therefore, do not hold anyone back because doing so would only force you to become stagnant yourself.

Imagine you have a tiny rat running around and then you step on its tail to prevent it from going. For as long as you keep on stepping on its tail, you

71

remain in the same position. That is the exact thing that you do to yourself and the people that you keep back. You prevent yourselves from exploring the world and making it your own kitchen to cook the greatness within you.

Everyone has a purpose and a period in their life, which is one of the difficult truths that I have learned to accept. The moment their purpose becomes fulfilled and their time in your life is up, then they would have to go. Despite your best efforts, they would eventually have to leave. Instead of sticking together and rotting together, I would prefer to let that friend and I go our separate ways so that we may still make a significant contribution to each other's lives in the future.

The world is like a big ocean with every one of us, like fishes in the big ocean. What happens in the ocean? Different fishes swim in different directions. Sometimes, they swim alongside each other and sometimes they swim alone. Either of the situations is solely dependent on the season and the kind of fish. However, learn to accept seasons and know your fish.

Rise Together!

It is not a suggestion but an instruction to you, my friend, to rise together. When you understand and define the essence of every relationship, it becomes easier for you to rise together with other people. High School becomes more interesting when you and your mates excel together. The school develops into a place of growth and development when one student excels in sports, the other in academics, and so forth.

Take a look at how insects function; they dare to ascend as a group. Given how little they are, it is surprising to see how well-organized and structured their manner of existence is. Each bee in a colony performs a specific task, and together, they all work to strengthen the colony.

We need to stop this competitive mindset that we have designed in our minds. Rather than starting pointless competitions, let us come together to grow ourselves and then our world.

CHAPTER 7

o · · · · · · · · o

TAKE TO
INITIATIVES

"Students must have initiative; they should not be mere imitators. They must learn to think and act for themselves - and be free."
— **Cesar Chavez**

Every human has the potential for reasoning. The brain as it is, solely, is designed for the purpose of thinking, the interpretation of thoughts, ideas, and many more complex capabilities. As such, when you take away a man's ability to reason, you have ultimately reduced him to a mere shell of the person he was before. The strength of every human lies in the power of discernment; for it is the greatest strength that every human is entitled to, by the virtue of our nature. Biologically, that is what has kept us at the top of the hierarchy of living things. Therefore, ask anyone what differentiates a man from a goat, and ninety percent of the responses acquired will be based on the fact that human beings can think while goats cannot.

American philosopher, Elbert Hubbard, offered an intriguing definition of initiative, when he remarked, "Initiative is doing the right thing without being told." My direct exposure to this phrase intrigued me because I began to reflect on the things I had accomplished on my own. How often do you behave morally when you are not being instructed or supervised? Make your own judgment regarding your level of initiative now.

I believe initiative is built on a foundation of responsibility. Few High School students are responsible enough to diligently prepare for their final examinations as soon as the school year begins. While some students will try to memorize the twelve to thirteen weeks' worth of study materials when the tests are just a day or two away. Because of this, many people are able to discern between playtime and study time, but this is not always the case.

*"Thoughts have power; thoughts are energy. And you can make your world or break it by your own thinking." – **Susan L. Taylor***

If you can eat, then, it shows you can think. And once you can think, then you should be able to design a path that is right for yourself. You have what it takes to be the best you can ever be in life. All you need to do is simply make a decision and choose to make it happen.

Are you taking initiative in other aspects of your life apart from school? It is really important that you do. The story of Mikaila Ulmer ought to inspire every young individual to start acting independently. It is incredible that a little child would consider opening a lemonade stand after experiencing bee stings. You must learn to find opportunities in every distress; triumph in setbacks and excellence in difficulties. That serves as the link for setting higher standards, proactively.

Think Positively!

If there is anything that I learned in 2021, it is the power of keeping a positive mindset. It works! The ability to think the 'YES' way when it is evident that everything is going the 'NO' way is capable of working wonders for you beyond your wildest imagination. When you think optimistically, you are able to take initiative because the ability to take initiative is meant for those who see light at the end of every tunnel.

Many amazing landmarks, and structures around the world today, including structures underwater, self-driving cars, and overhead bridges, are all examples of how a man can act decisively when he recognizes a possibility in the face of an impossibility. Although the idea of homes or bridges being above or below water, at some point, seemed somewhat absurd, they are all around us today. Therefore, whenever you choose to see the silver lining of life and become innovative, you can do more and be more.

Great ideas become more realistic only when the mind is relieved, and not when it is gloomy or burdened. A good way to rid the mind of burdens is to think positive thoughts. So, why not see the potential in every situation and leverage them into building something awe-inspiring? Because perfection resides within you, I am confident that all you need is to plant that seed, and something truly magnificent will grow out of you.

"Once you replace negative thoughts with positive ones, you will start getting positive results," were the words attributed to Willie Nelson. Because initiative is what births greatness, it follows that positive attitudes beget positive results. It is amusing to watch plants go about their daily activities in peace as you stare at them. Because of their calm environment, they were able to use the intense heat to produce food through photosynthesis.

Like plants, it is essential for you to overcome challenging circumstances with graceful, and optimistic thinking so that you can take action to improve yourself and make a meaningful contribution to the world.

Problems Need Solutions

There will always be problems in the world. Although it is a somber fact, it is, nevertheless, true. The consoling prospect is that each problem can be solved, with a unique solution. What makes the most sense is that, provided you choose to embrace innovation, you can contribute to developing a solution to one of these many problems. People who stand out are those who provide solutions to problems because the world is in dire need of such solutions.

A man saw that people needed a faster way to communicate with their loved ones who were thousands of miles away from them, and then innovated networking. How did he act? He created the telephone! The beauty of solutions is that they evolve! After the telephone was created, the mobile phone followed, and our commitment to finding effective solutions led us all the way to the era of Social media. Who knows, maybe in the near future someone would create something even more effective and mind-boggling than social media. That someone could be you.

There are some issues right now that you are the solution to. If there is a problem with littering in your classroom, for instance, you might start by properly disposing of your trash; in this case, you would be a large part of the solution. Being the answer demonstrates your capacity to take initiative and be innovative. It establishes you as a leader with exceptional abilities. Recalling Elbert Hubbard's perspective on taking initiative, you can see from his comments that you should solve problems rather than cause them.

When you assess a situation, what is your reaction to it? How do you manage such circumstances? Do you become the problem or the solution? These are basically questions every young person should ask themselves since it will give them an idea of where they currently stand.

Own Your Choices

Being able to take ownership of your own decisions is a very distinctive aspect of being proactive, and taking initiative. Every young person experiences a period in their lives when they clamor for independence, and this is the essence of independence: accepting responsibility for your actions, whether or not they benefit you. Some children in a conference were asked if they had ever felt bad about doing something that their parents had forbidden them from doing. Guess what? Almost no one, even the grown-ups present, offered a response.

You see, very few individuals can handle the guilt of having to live with the consequences of their actions, and that is where true maturity resides.

Many people find it hard to do the right thing, even when it is placed in front of them. And when the repercussions get more severe, they get scared and lay the blame on their teachers, parents, or friends. As a matter of fact, that is by no means taking responsibility, at all; in fact, it is just the opposite. You are expected to guide your decisions and deal with whatever results from them.

Many of us have made messes that cannot be cleaned, and of course, this doesn't mean we have failed. However, we have to make new decisions and do better. When I was a student, we were conducting a titration experiment in the Chemistry Lab. In High School, I conducted a number of titration studies, so I was pretty familiar with the procedure. I was done with my experiment and I saw this particular student who apparently was doing the wrong thing, so I approached her and asked her what she thought. Her response surprised me. "Thank you Charles, but I am here to learn so I will fail a few times and eventually get it," she said to me.

It is baffling to observe that not many students are willing to own their actions. The majority of pupils want an easy way out of school and life in general. Your initiative is your choice, therefore own it, whether it turned out to be wise or not. The best thing you can do is go back and make things right.

Be Proactive

Being proactive is one of the fundamentals of taking initiative. That is why a wise person would literally have done the right thing before others even considered it. The human mind is structured in such a way that it is able to think ahead once you activate it to do so. You may occasionally be required to see the future before anyone else does. It is a very effective technique to make plans in advance and be ready for the unexpected. Instead of trying to stop the damage from happening, it is wiser to take action before the need arises for them.

When you think about it, being proactive is a fantastic antidote to procrastination. You continue to procrastinate because you have not made the decision to take the initiative. Procrastination is unnecessary when you are proactive; the task would have already been completed to avoid any delay.

Another benefit of being proactive is that you have the chance to pursue other endeavors that call for more focus while still carrying them out to the best of your abilities. Specific circumstances call for specific actions. You have the luxury of time to handle these situations diplomatically whenever they come because you are not preoccupied with a ton of other tasks.

As a student, you may find yourself entangled in the web of extra-curricular activities, sports, and academics. However, if you want to succeed in all areas, certain things will undoubtedly require more attention, so you must make sure that you take on some tasks first so that you have enough time to concentrate on what requires special attention.

I had a very hectic schedule back in high school. I had to leave campus as late as 5 PM and at 6 PM on some days. When I eventually assumed the highest leadership position among students, it became almost uncontrollable. In 9th grade, I was meant to be taking a break since the junior High School examinations had just ended, but I had to go to class to get ready for a state debate tournament. My mother had to wait for almost two hours before she could come to pick me up from school.

I had to constantly try to keep up while dealing with days like this. Nonetheless, the truth about excellence remains that it may be tough to manage because everything demands your attention simultaneously, and all are important.

The average CEO of a Fortune 500 company makes sure to complete the 'irrelevant' activity when time starts to run out. Therefore, cultivate the culture of doing what you will call 'irrelevant' when the time looks like it will be wasted on frivolities.

I have always adhered to the idea that "suffering now will lead to pleasure later." In light of this, I made an effort to make sure that I would never again let my schedule become filled up due to time wastage. The principle of prioritizing that I discussed earlier, works in synchrony with being proactive. As such, make sure you inculcate both.

Have Foresight

Being able to see things that others can or cannot see can be really cool. It serves as evidence of how unhinged your mind can get; yes, unhinged. Because life rarely gives us the chance to see beyond our physical eyes, it takes guts to be foresighted. However, only those who are able to see beyond the scope of their physical vision are able to scale mountains. Although physical sight is strong, inner sight is stronger because it determines the level of success you achieve in life.

The definition of "foresight" is, seeing clearer, and sharply even before your physical eyes see. How far can you see? There is no initiative without foresight because you cannot think until your sense of sight is coordinated. The essence of foresight in elevating men can never be overemphasized. It has benefited countless individuals and will continue to do so for many more.

"Humans are somewhat endowed with the gift of foresight. Nevertheless, we frequently acquire knowledge through failure," stated David Grinspoon. It's interesting how most people just realize how much money they've lost as a result of their lack of vision. Although, it is often true that "experience is the best teacher," this is not always the case. Before understanding a mistake, you don't need to endure something traumatic. You can use your ability to see things ahead of time to start picturing them right away.

You don't have to miss that opportunity before realizing that you could have invested it. You do not have to fail a course before knowing that you could have met a friend to study what you did not understand. Activate your inner sight because even a blind man with a powerful sight within will be greater than a thousand men with 20/20 vision.

Be Independent

Eighty percent of young adults in our world today desire some form of self-independence when they turn sixteen. They want the freedom to date, select their careers, meet new people and go anywhere in the world. In some exceptional cases, they believe they are old enough to live independently.

They simply want to explore life and experience what adulthood feels like. At this stage of their lives, they behave quite impulsively, because they find it simpler to break the law than to follow it. They could find comfort in situations they would often never wish to find themselves in, and they tend to be much ruder to elderly people. The good news is that wanting to be or being independent are both perfectly acceptable. You may have heard the term "youthful exuberance," but I won't use that term. Like I said earlier, that is very natural. One thing about youthful exuberance, however, is that it gives you the impression that you are free when, in reality, bound by the laws of society. So once again, you get to make that decision!

Independence, in an actual sense, requires you to be responsible for your actions and whatever choices you make. It is the very foundation upon which taking initiative is built. As candid as it might sound, you have to learn to be independent, especially when making some decisions that could decide how your life turns out. Decisions like this could be whether you follow a STEM or Arts & Humanities pathway in high school; whether or not you are emotionally mature to date; or how you choose to respond to circumstances, like if you suddenly discovered you were adopted.

When we find ourselves in unpleasant situations; instead of resisting them, we should learn to overcome them. Your ability to be independent will be demonstrated when you learn how to handle ups and downs.

Even if they wanted to, parents and teachers can't always be there, so you have to learn how to handle your life the proper way, with or without them. Not everything requires you to run to your parents or teachers for help. So many virtues have done a terrific job in articulating what the correct standards are since society has established standards for us. Your ability to determine whatever standard(s) to uphold is what you have the most control and power over.

It's a difficult thing to accept, but you won't be independent and even if you try, you'll approach independence incorrectly unless you accept that you will always pay for your decisions. But keep in mind that you can only take initiative once you are independent.

Take Action

In as much as it is fundamental to take initiative, your success depends entirely on you getting up and doing something. Some people have some of the best ideas, but because they never act on them, it seems as though they had nothing to contribute. Until you express what is inside of you, no one will know.

The world's a stage for everyone to put forward his or her own stunt and the only person that can limit yours is you. Many people have died with the best ideas buried deep inside of them and they could not contribute their little quota to the world because they decided to conceal what was hidden inside of them. There is a reason behind why humans were charged to procreate, and dominate the earth. It is because man is expected to bring forth that seed that has been buried inside of him.

Many people have passed away with their best ideas tucked away inside of them, unable to make their own small contribution to the world because they chose to keep their innovations to themselves.

Take this to heart: Do not ever be scared of speaking up or taking action. Again, you might be just who the world needs to solve that long-existing problem.

Did You Fail? Get Up, And Get Back At It!

We are all aware of the devastation that failure can cause—having your GPA plummet, not getting into your desired college, failing to make the varsity team despite practicing all year, and more. It demoralizes you and damages your self-esteem.

What's worse is that making progress after a significant failure is not any simpler. Nevertheless, you cannot let it stop you from moving forward and living a fulfilling life. It's crucial to learn how to pick yourself up after a fall and move on from failure.

It is never simple to succeed. Before becoming great, you will have to stumble a few times. Before you can swim well, you might need to come dangerously close to drowning numerous times. The only thing you must never stop doing is trying.

Come to think of it, failure might not be so bad if it makes you fearless and you ultimately succeed.

I can't even begin to count how many times I've felt like a failure. Even in those trying times, I never gave the thought to agree that I am a failure because, in reality, I am not and never will be, and the same is true of you.

Examples include entering a competition with high expectations and coming in last place, receiving a really poor grade on a test you worked so hard to prepare for, losing your father at a young age, and being forced to wait a year after high school to enroll in college.

Give your critics a run for their money while making your perceived failures the best thing to ever happen to you. Do you know what types of stories people enjoy hearing? It is made up of people who at first failed before rising to their feet and succeeding. For many others out there, the picking up part is always a major source of inspiration. So, friend, make your failure awesome today to serve as inspiration.

Begin To Fly

It is truly amazing to see the wonderful things that are created as a result of someone taking the initiative and making their ideas known. Make up your mind that "I am the world's smartest, most intelligent, and most brilliant person." I'll soar higher than I ever imagined when the time comes.

As long as you keep talking positively to yourself and participating in the discourse, you will discover that you could be the next person to solve one of the biggest problems in the world. My friend, soar as high as you can because your path to greatness is an unending one.

CHAPTER 8

o · · · · · · · · · o

WHEN LIFE TURNS
SOUR

"You should never view your challenges as a disadvantage. Instead, you need to understand that your experience facing and overcoming adversity is one of your biggest advantages."
– Michelle Obama

The cliche statement, "Life is not a bed of roses," shows how true it is that life is no easy game. Sometimes life will seem like a bed of roses, and some other times, a death sentence. Perhaps some young people decided to escape the reality of life through drug abuse or suicide. But life does not work that way. People who put in the work are the ones who succeed. They keep on fighting for the life they want and choose never to quit. That is how to live.

I was born into a home where I got anything I wanted. Everything was at my beck and call. Life was exciting, and most of my mates envied me. Our house was filled with love, joy, peace, and all the good things in life. No visitor ever left our place empty-handed because we always had more than enough to give. We never lacked nor borrowed. We lived in abundance.

In March 2009, my dad died of an illness that lasted about three weeks. Funny how such a brief period was enough to end the life of a bright family man with a promising future. The entire family was devastated. My brother, Emma, and I were still young; I was five years old, and Emma was three. So I barely recall what happened and was clueless about everything. I can only remember seeing people lower my dad into a grave.

I remember that at the funeral, everybody was sad, and my mum was crying profusely. Emma often says, "they put my dad in a box and covered him with sand." We were too naive to realize that we would have to continue our lives without a father. Whenever we asked about our dad's whereabouts, people would tell us that he traveled to heaven and was coming back soon. Later as we grew older, we realized that no one returns from a journey to heaven.

March 2009 events affected our lives a bit. In December of that same year, we moved to our own house, a duplex with six bedrooms, two sitting rooms, a study, and a lounge, where the three of us lived with a maid. My mum stopped welcoming visitors and distant relatives because she could not bear the hurt. A young woman who enjoyed less than seven years of marriage decided not to remarry. Many people found her decision shocking, and most wondered how she would cope.

We went on with our lives as a family without a dad. My mum played mother and father roles in our lives and still took care of her managerial duties as a banker. She showered us with love, care, spiritual and financial support, and every good thing that children with both parents enjoyed. Today, she remains my most loved person because she has done what a thousand parents cannot do.

Things were great for us until we got into a financial crisis in November 2015. I was in my second year of junior high school while my brother was still in elementary school. We were troubled and had no idea how to survive, but we wanted to pull through with God. I remained determined to become successful because I knew I was destined for greatness, and it does not come easy.

We were harassed many times in school because of outstanding tuition fees. Schools nowadays care more about money than their students' well-being, so I was not surprised. Regardless, we kept on pushing. I always had my hopes high because I knew that one day I would tell the world my story like I am right now.

Why am I sharing these stories with you? I want you to know that no matter what you are going through, someone has been in your shoes before. Some people have been through worse and still came out victorious because everyone should win. Winners take advantage of difficult situations to bring out the best in them. Tell yourself, "I am a winner."

The determination to make it

Determination is the stepping stone to success. Wherever there is a will, there will always be a way. Renowned writer and speaker Og Mandino once said, "Failure will never overtake me if my determination to succeed is strong enough." I love those words because they are like a mantra every young person should recite when they wake up in the morning.

Having the will to make it helps one create a bright future. Like me, many others have had it rough in life, but I decided to keep forging ahead, not minding the bumps on the road. One of my mentors, Sylvester Jenkins, shared his story in his book, 'A quick cure to Successful Leadership.'

He grew up in a low-income, single-parent home in a ghetto in Columbus, an environment brutal enough to turn anyone into anything other than good. He said, "The odds were stacked against my siblings and me." Like many young folks, he joined a gang at thirteen and began to indulge in drug use. However, there was a turning point when he realized he wanted more for himself. Today, he is an army veteran and an expert in resilient leadership.

I do not know your resolve, nor do I know what situation is challenging you. But whatever you are going through, I want you to know that you are made for more. You are to stun the world and be successful.

Life will not always be easy, even if it may be for you now. There will be roadblocks along the way, regardless of how you started your journey. But with diligence, dedication, and most importantly, determination, you will reach the top. The journey of life is like a ladder. If you are not great at climbing, like me, you should never look down if you want to make progress.

So, stop looking down. You have no business with what happens beneath you but everything before you. Fight for your place at the top of the ladder because you belong there. Success is your entitlement, not your ambition, so take your spot at the top.

Tommy Lasorda said, "the difference between the impossible and the possible lies in a man's determination." Simply put, your level of determination determines how far you go in life.

Define your situations

Do not allow your situations to define you. Yes, some people are victims of their circumstances. But yours is to turn your circumstance to your advantage. Bill Gates once said, "If you were born poor, it is not your fault, but if you die poor, it is your mistake."

Behind every challenge lies true success, but no one emerges a victor without hurdles. Henceforth, begin to see every opposition as your source of strength to become a better version of yourself and to prepare for the greater good. Do not forget that the orange fruit tastes sour before it becomes sweet.

So, friend, accept your 'sour' and make it 'sweet.' Stop stressing over how someone else went through the same situation with a different result. Your obstacles should never dampen your spirit but reveal the lion in you. In the business of raising bars, you have to exploit situations and not brood over them to produce excellence.

Great men rise from tough times. I will never stop admiring Ben Carson's story. I was thrilled to see how someone who was in a hopeless life situation decided to define his circumstance and eventually amounted to greatness.

Think again about Bill Gates' words and reflect on circumstances you did not bring upon yourself. It could be having to grow up with a single parent, living with a health condition, or being born into a poor home. None of those things is your fault. But one thing is sure - you can change them and rise above them.

A bee stung Mikaila Ulmer. A bee's sting is poisonous enough to hospitalize a person, but that bee sting birthed a fast-growing lemonade company. She undoubtedly practiced the proverb that states, "when life gives you lemons, make lemonade," except that hers was a bee sting. A man fails because of his inability to rise above his situation. Once he can overshadow his problems, he becomes successful.

Never give up

I believe you can raise many bars if you choose never to give up and never to lose hope. Most self-taught mentors accentuate the concept of not quitting and have done great, emphasizing the need to keep striving. The ball is now in your court whether to use these teachings or not.

Let me ask you: why should you give up? People use a proven technique when they feel like giving up, and it will benefit you whenever you find yourself in a similar situation. Take a pen and paper and list reasons why you should give up on whatever it is. Then, on another side of the sheet, list reasons you should not give up.

You will see that the first list will have very few bullet points, while the other may even be endless. Do you know why? It is because there are a million reasons why you should keep going. I accepted the Turkish proverb, "this too shall pass," because everything is a function of time, and at the right time, things will be better.

Jack Ma's words, "never give up. Today is hard, tomorrow will be worse, but the day after tomorrow will be sunshine," are so comforting. There is light at the end of the tunnel. The road may be long, dark, and narrow, but eventually, there will be hope.

As sour as it sounds, giving up only makes you the biggest loser. You are stronger than your problems, but you can only prove that to the world when you succeed. If I had given up years ago, I might have never written this impactful book for you, my dear friend. I chose to keep fighting through tough times and emerged a conqueror. You can turn out a victor if you do not give up.

Time will tell

When we had it rough in life, my mother would assure us that "time will tell." Indeed, time did tell. Now, I am advancing my education in one of the most prestigious colleges in New Jersey, United States. You are reading my first book, and more is to come. I am well-paid at my job and happy.

Everything in life is a function of time. There is a time for pain and one for joy. Perhaps this is your time of struggle; you should know that joy is coming. Always remember that God's time remains the best, and while man has many proposals, everything is under God's disposal.

Why does the sun shine not at night and the moon appear not during the day? They are programmed to appear at a set time. And until that moment comes, they remain hidden in the sky. So, while you keep pushing, remember there is time for everything.

Also, your level of preparedness comes to play. Sometimes, certain things fail to happen to us because we are not prepared enough for them. One instance is of a five-year-old child requesting his father's car keys to drive his car. No matter how much the kid thinks he knows, he cannot get the keys from his father because his father knows that his son is not ready to handle a car.

Sometimes, like that kid, we desire car keys, and it may seem like the world is against us when we do not get what we want. But we fail to acknowledge that the one who sees all things knows we are unprepared. No one goes to war unready, so consider now your preparation time and go with the flow.

If I had been too hasty with certain things, I might have become unsuccessful. Losing my father at a tender age forced me to become very mature while facing a financial crisis. That experience developed into a good business sense for me. Today, I possess a natural, strong passion for business leadership.

All will be well before you know it, and you will live your dream life. Just keep pushing with high hopes of your success. Your season is coming where you will reap your harvest. Keep on sowing good seeds now so that your harvest will be bountiful.

Be thankful

I am always grateful for life. It is one of the many lessons my faith has imbued in me, and I never get tired of it. Being appreciative is comforting. I once told someone, "be thankful for the little you have before wishing for bigger things." The world is experiencing unspeakable vices because the perpetrators are not grateful for what they have.

You see, you will eventually become greedy if you are never appreciative. When you start to desire things you can not afford and are ready to acquire those things illicitly, then you must search your heart for criminal tendencies. Everything on earth is vain, and I want you to see it as such. I am privileged to have an aunt working in a nursing home who tells me how people die every day regardless of how much they have.

Success is desirable. But any achievement that will make you eat at your conscience is not worth it. Greatness comes in many forms other than wealth, fame, or influence. You can be great just by putting a smile on people's faces. Give alms to beggars, and you will realize that excellence does not always come big. Be thankful for what you have.

What should you be grateful for? Appreciate your life, your family, the shelter over your head, the food you eat, and everything you have. Let me shock you. Your current situation is someone else's desire. Also, you cannot advance in life when you do not value your present state.

When Melody Beattie said, "Gratitude makes sense of our past, brings peace for today, and creates a vision for tomorrow," she must have experienced the healing power of gratitude. I heard about a woman who became one of the greatest American authors. She started drinking at 12, and by 18 years old, she had already become a drug addict.

Her biography showed that she is a survivor of abandonment, kidnapping, and drug abuse. Her neighbor abused her sexually, and her husband drained her finances. Everything got worse when her son died in a skiing accident. However, Melody found peace, and today she is grateful for life. Her decision helped her publish over fifteen books in twenty years, and she has helped millions of people globally find peace.

Remember that every hovering cloud has a silver lining and some good in every negative situation. Also, know that God wants you to appreciate your current position so that he can lift you to a realm of overabundant exploits. You will soon experience your season of celebration, so always keep your heart full of thanks.

The best is coming

Friend, better days are ahead of you whether you know it or not. Now might seem like the worst phase of your life, but I assure you that your best is still coming. Let every day be a day of gratitude for you because you never know when the clock strikes your time. You should enter your season of lifting with happiness.

Every successful person has been through struggles before coming into the limelight. They are products of their wise decisions to keep pushing, and today, the world celebrates them. If I can be successful, then you can too.

CHAPTER 9

○ · · · · · · · · ○

YOU DON'T HAVE
ALL-DAY

"Time is more valuable than money. You can get more money, but you cannot get more time."
– Jim Rohn

Since no one has control over time but it has a greater value than many of the things we all strive for, the importance of time management cannot be overstated. I had the honor of conducting a survey for work on the health and successful aging of adults between the ages of forty and eighty. The survey's final question asks you to rank your life on a scale of one to ten. The median response received was in the range of five to six.

More than anything, the average septuagenarian yearns for more time. As one gets older, they want more time to accomplish more things. Time is a fundamental aspect of human existence that hasn't changed since the beginning of time, just like change. Knowing that we only have twenty-four hours in a day that lasts for 365 days to accomplish great deeds hurts. Knowing that I can accomplish anything when I put the time to good use is personally quite comforting.

24 hours is just enough time to gain notoriety. It can happen that quickly. I've come to understand that it only takes a single second to reach the top, after which your life will never be the same. After ascending several stairs, you only need one more to reach the last floor. The key takeaway from this is that you need to manage your time effectively if you want to accomplish a lot in a short amount of time.

It is not only students who have trouble using their time effectively. Actually, everybody does! The thing is because nobody has all day, some people have made conscious efforts to avoid wasting time. You only have twenty-four hours to raise the bar before tomorrow arrives and another one needs to be

It's funny how tomorrow never comes. Only today, which has passed, and yesterday, remain for you to change things. Mother Teresa once said that "although tomorrow has not yet arrived, yesterday is gone". We only have today. Let's get going.

According to Steve Harvey, if you get eight hours of sleep per day, know that you've slept for one-third of your life. Now let me analyze a typical high school student's life. From Monday through Friday, you spend a minimum of six hours in school. You spend roughly eight hours a day sleeping and three hours a day studying. You now have about seven more hours free to do whatever you want, including hanging out with friends, playing games, watching movies, eating, and relaxing.

I'll say no more than that, but be aware that using your time efficiently is different from simply spending it.

Time waits for no one. Either you make use of it while you have it or you live the rest of your life feeling guilty for wasting it. You will always have the freedom of choice. You are currently in your youth. Now is the time to make wise use of your time by putting it toward worthwhile endeavors. There is nothing wrong with you enjoying yourself and having fun. I'm a big believer in doing what makes you happy to be happy, but it's also crucial to make sure that whatever makes you happy is something you can look back on and proudly say, "Yes! I did that."

There is time for everything

Making decisions that will have an impact on how effectively you manage your time will be greatly influenced by your awareness that everything has its proper time and season. There is a time and season for everything under the sun. Perhaps this explains why some things we long for only materialize when they are meant to.

You are an actor on earth, and I want you to understand and accept that. Your destiny is your play, and the world is your stage. You are now free to interpret your script and play out your role however you see fit. How well you have utilized your time on earth will be determined by that. In high school, where you only have six years to complete before entering college, which is a taste of the real world, it is similar.

One of my two friends who graduated from high school at the same time as I said he missed high school so much when we spoke a while back. He found that college, which is a simulation of the real world, was moving a little too fast for him, and that it was difficult for him to keep up. There is a time for everything, I simply replied to him. It's time for you to mature and become a man. Enjoy it because it will serve as your new normal for the foreseeable future.

You have 4-6 years of high school to complete, depending on what part of the world you're in. You can write your name in gold in that amount of time easily. If you can't get through this time, you probably won't be able to manage your time well in college. Nobody is waiting for the world. The world is not at all suitable for babies because it is hard. It is intended for those who recognize the season and make the most of it.

The issue you are having is not a lack of time, but rather that you spend your time on things that you shouldn't be. You should develop the ability to act appropriately at all times. That shows obedience to your destiny as well as to whoever it is that is establishing the rules. So, submit to your fate.

What will happen when you have to work from eight to five or run your business, then you have a family and kids to take care of, you have elderly parents to take care of, you have commitments here and there, and you are complaining that you don't have time when half of your entire life is being run by other people?

There is enough time for you to work, rest, and study, as well as to play and have fun. All you have to do is focus your energy in the right direction at the right time to complete all of the things that life requires of you.
The power of prioritizing

In Brian Tracy's book 'Eat that Frog,' he identified the most important and challenging tasks that people have to attend to and he advised that it is important to finish these tasks first. You can start identifying the frogs you have and make thoughtful preparations for how you intend to eat them. You see, setting priorities is a good way to complete tasks more quickly and easily.

According to a business principle known as the "Pareto 80/20 principle," 80% of your inputs will ultimately determine your outputs. Now let's apply that idea to time management in a slightly different way. You should make a list of all your tasks each day and then divide them into two groups. The two must be 80 percent different from one another.

The most important tasks should be the title of the first group, which comprises 20% of the total, and the tasks that should be completed should be the title of the second group. The concept here is that the list of things you MUST complete is in the 20% group. While the other group refers to things that should be done, they are the more difficult and time-consuming tasks that demand a significant investment of time. If you don't complete them, it won't cause you a serious setback.

For instance, 20% of your time might be spent on a Chemistry research project that must be finished and turned in by the end of the week, while 80% of your time might be spent planning a hangout with your friends. This is something that can be accomplished mentally, and with the advancement of technology, you can do it with your phone.

As an alternative, always carry a pocket note and a pen with you. I always carry a pocket note and a pen with me wherever I go, including the gym, so I can jot down tasks I need to complete and cross them off. An organized life gives you a head start on reaching your goals because an organized person finds it simpler to live by principles, obey rules, stay focused, and maintain equilibrium. One of the foundational elements of leading an organized life is prioritizing.

YOLO!

Every young person wants to hear the phrase "You only live once," or "YOLO." As absurd as it may sound, it is the undisputed reality of life. Nobody has two lives at once. Everyone only has one journey on earth, and when that journey is over, everything ends. As a result, you should enjoy yourself, but not at the expense of other more crucial things.

According to Mark Twain, you will regret the things you didn't do more than the ones you did in twenty years. Therefore, remove the bowlines. Leave the safe harbor and set sail. Use the trade winds to your advantage. Explore. Dream and learn. It is amazing to hear those words because they serve as a reminder that we only have one life, so we must enjoy it while we are here.

Spend your time doing things that are good for you and bring you joy without necessarily causing harm to others. I love the Abba song "Dancing Queen" because it constantly reminds me that it's time for me to enjoy myself. You are having the time of your life, but you don't have all day to enjoy it, my friend.

Meet with family, hang out with friends, visit various tourist attractions, play games, and only get involved in enjoyable activities that make you happy. Your children will eventually inquire about your childhood. You don't want to wish you had gone on a roller coaster when you were younger while watching them ride one. Additionally, you don't want to be a dull parent with no amusing or exciting stories to share with your children.

I remember the first time I went fishing, I vowed to buy a fishing rod because I had so much fun. Also, the first time I went kayaking, it was so much fun. All these experiences remain fresh in my mind and will remain with me for life. You should take some time out for recreation and relaxation. It is needed for your mental health.

Don't just pass through the school, let the school pass through you

Because you don't have forever to spend in high school, it is wise to spend quality time letting the good of your school's environment infiltrate you. During some of the school assemblies, our Vice-principal academics would emphasize the need to let the school pass through us individually.

You are spending a great portion of your years on earth within the four walls of high school. Consequently, that time must count so that in years to come, you can look back and call yourself an achiever. Time is fundamental in making kings but kings who are produced from time, are people who endeavor to make use of time and eventually make an impact.

Albert Einstein said that education is not the learning of facts but the training of the mind to think. The day you graduate from high school, ask yourself one question 'Can I think now?' Your sincere response to that question will help you ascertain whether education has left an indelible mark on you. It is not just about carrying a big bag with many books for five days a week and returning home with little or nothing to show for it.

Use your time in school as effectively as possible. Take part in all endeavors that will foster and bring forth the excellence that resides within you. Your parents have invested a sizable sum of money in your education because they want you to outperform them in all facets of life. Since excellence is your birthright, you must make the world aware of it.

Keep calm and get rejuvenated

The proverb "all work and no play makes Jack a dull boy" is absolutely true. You see, it pays just as much to be stable mentally and physically as it does to be active and put your energy to good use. Every time Sylvester Jenkins, my mentor, and I speak on the phone, he always wants to know how I'm doing mentally. He introduced me to the canteens of life and frequently stresses the importance of the mental canteen for success.

The beginning of quality time management is when you know how to manage your time enough to set out sufficient time to rest and lay your mind. Rest and sleep are food to the soul. Nowadays, several people come up with different theories telling you that to be successful, you should sleep for less than five hours a day and so on. Personally, I find some of those theories appalling because I know that the teachers of these false nuggets sleep the longest every day.

Spend time relaxing, sleeping, and engaging in activities that will stabilize your mind, body, and soul. Raising bars requires thinking, and thinking requires a calm mind, so only someone who is mentally stable can do it.

Since my mind is most peaceful at night, that is when I tend to write and complete important tasks, but it in no way interferes with my sleep or rest time. I make it a point to find some downtime.

Yes, you must put in a lot of study time if you want to succeed academically, but do not sacrifice your mental well-being in the process. To claim that you are studying to the point where you have eye bags or constant headaches is unreasonable.

I had the good fortune to be part of a highly competitive group where everyone strived for excellence. Many of us were forced to push ourselves past our limits by this. I observed that my eyes were constantly sore, and I began to experience severe headaches. Sometimes I had trouble focusing in class, and I was eager for the end of the school year because I was exhausted. I used to get up as early as 5 am and leave for school on Lagos Road by 6 am. The school nurse then gave me some advice, and I stopped. I found that when I rested more and balanced my time, things started to improve. I improved my effectiveness and output.

Discipline in time management

People who manage their twenty-four hours the best are highly disciplined. They make schedules and adhere to them while living their lives. They are very productive because they are not reluctant to say "No" when it is necessary. Sometimes, being disciplined is all you need; it's not about exhausting yourself. In actuality, discipline is the cornerstone of effective time management.

You are unable to live a coordinated life if you cannot establish standards for yourself that you adhere to. Have you ever questioned why some powerful people retain personal assistants? It is necessary for coordination, which comes only from discipline. The good news is that you don't need a personal assistant to be organized; you just need to be disciplined.

How do you deal with interruptions and unusual situations? Keep in mind that you don't have to always make a person happy by agreeing to go on dates—whether they are play dates, movie dates, picnic dates, or other types of outings. Adopt discipline! Be able to say "no" and use your time wisely. Now is the time to work hard so that you can later enjoy yourself.

Imagine having to put in efforts now and then succeeding and never having to suffer again or enjoying to the fullest now and living the rest of your life toiling hard for every meal. The choice is yours to make!

CHAPTER 10

○ · · · · · · · · ○

IT IS ALL ON
GOD

"God never ends anything on a negative; God always ends on a positive."
– Edwin Louis Cole

There is always the God factor behind every success. No matter how some successful people try to attribute their success to their efforts, God remains the lifter and elevator of men. My high school story will never be complete without me acknowledging God's role in raising me. Everyone runs the RACE of life, but when you invite God to help you, it becomes GRACE, and it takes grace to accelerate to any height in life.

I was privileged by grace to know Christ at a tender age. When I was young, some people called me a pastor because of how mature I usually prayed. The first time I got called to lead the assembly in high school was a couple of weeks into year seven. I began calling some of the names of God while praying to him and the whole school started laughing. What seemed like an embarrassing situation soon turned out to favor me, as I became admired by teachers and students alike.

However, deep inside me, I never felt like a pastor, and to date, I still do not. The difference between then and now is I have become more conscious and guided in my walk with God, and I am benefiting from it greatly. I once said to God, "Lord, you do not even wait for me to pray again before you provide." I rededicated my life to Jesus several years ago, after taking the prayer to be born again, at various Christian meetings.

Now let me tell you what led me to take that decision. I was doing well, but I felt unfulfilled. To crown it all, I was friends with a very toxic and depressed individual whom I usually tried to help feel better with empathy. It was a harmful decision as the thought of suicide almost crossed my mind once. Then, I knew I needed help. As a result, I spoke to one of my good friends, Imim. I told him I wanted to rededicate my life to Jesus, and he led me through the process.

It has been some years now, and I am basking in the glory of the Lord. It has been a delightful and pleasurable journey, walking with God wholeheartedly. Do I still make mistakes? Yes! But I have learned to identify my weaknesses and avoid them. What is the secret?

Jesus saith unto him, I am the way, the truth, and the life: no man cometh unto the Father, but by me.
— John 14:6 (KJV)

That is my secret, Jesus. I have fathomed that if I desire a remarkable ascent to the top, then Jesus must be at the center of it all. You must submit totally to his will for your life.

God is just so wonderful. One would absolutely love to attribute as many things as possible to the majesty and splendor of the great creator. Everything on earth, including birds, animals, plants, rivers, oceans, people, and everything else that exists. Isn't it amazing how great God is?

There is a song titled: "Creator of the universe," and I love that song so much. It describes the mighty power of Jesus. If you are ready to go anywhere, you should trust in Jesus and not your abilities. Take note of the difference between 'anywhere' and 'somewhere.' Anyone going anywhere is without purpose, focus, vision, direction, and destination, but the man who goes somewhere has a destination.

We have heard stories of people who hit rock bottom, but when they found the Lord, he transformed them. Your success with God is sure when you are committed to following Him in a delightsome way.

Instructions Will Elevate You

God's word is yea and amen. He never minces his words because He only says what he means and he means everything he says. Consequently, His word is designed to be a light source to his children, by acting in four dimensions — For doctrine, for reproof, for correction, for instruction. 2 Timothy 3:16 says that

*All scripture is given by inspiration of God and is profitable for doctrine, reproof, correction, for instruction in righteousness. – **2 Timothy 3:16***

But of the four, there is one that stands out; "instruction." As long as the earth exists, instructions will remain superior to principles. While it's essential to live by principles to live a good life, instructions will make you live an accomplished life by setting you on high. God's words are practical instructions designed solely for profitable living. See Deuteronomy 28:1.

*And it shall come to pass, if thou shalt hearken diligently unto the voice of the LORD thy God, to observe and to do all his commandments which I command thee this day, that the LORD thy God will set thee on high above all nations of the earth – **Deuteronomy 28:1***

Now, if you go further down that chapter of the Bible, you will see those different kinds of blessings were listed through verse 13 and God still emphasized that to enjoy those blessings, we must follow his instructions in two verses of the chapter. God honors his word more than His name, so He is very interested in us following his instructions.

God is not wicked. He is not a taskmaster. He instructs us to do things that he has empowered us to do, like to give, show love, and honor him. His word remains the primary source of His guidelines, for His children to lead a prosperous life.

When I was entering high school, I was given a book; "Handbook for Learners," and I remember that in the 10th grade, I received the same book. It was the school's code of conduct for students. It included rules and regulations for students to follow. Do's and don'ts.

No student needed anyone to tell them that if they did anything contrary to the handbook, they would have themselves to blame. Some students defied it, nonetheless. During my stay in high school, I witnessed the expulsion of almost five students, and it was not a fun sight. I want you to always have something at the back of your mind – Your primary assignment in school is to learn and be successful in life, so don't joke with it. Walk with God, and you will achieve this.

God wants us to serve him with obedience to His commandments. When you do otherwise, you do not qualify for his blessings at all. It is just like you and your father. When your father is upset with you for disobeying a simple instruction, does he smile at you? How much more, the father of fathers? The

Almighty!

Cast your cares on him

The composer of one of the most sung hymns in the world today, Charles Albert Tindley, was born to a slave father and a free mother. He was uneducated, yet, he wrote the hymn 'Leave it there.' Is that not ironic? Well, that is how God raises men from the worst backgrounds. He is capable of bearing all your burdens if only you will allow him to carry them for you.

He will always be there for you and ready to help you. God is ever faithful and ever sure. Regardless of the negative perception you might have about yourself, He is always willing to receive you with open arms. Knowing that there is someone that you can run to in times of trouble is comforting.

The day I realized I could leave everything at Jesus' feet marked a turning point in my life. Nothing gives me sleepless nights. I have no concerns or worries because I rest assured that God will do it. In the year 2021, my slogan, whenever I found myself in troubled waters, was "God will do it," and he did it. He has never stopped doing it, and I will not stop casting my care on him.

When I discuss with someone, and I am told "Not to worry" about something, I tell them that I am never worried. I would say that I don't even worry about myself, so why should I worry about anything on earth. I sleep like a baby under his watch and wake up every morning like a victor.

As a high schooler, you will need Him, especially when things are not going as expected. Learn to rely on God and allow him to call the shots in your life because, with Him, your path will always be made clear.

Mysteries that engender excellence

I am not a preacher, but there are some principles that I live by, and I have been blessed by them ever since I began that lifestyle. These principles might seem ordinary, but they go a long way in making you prosper, not just in school but in life. Let us consider them:

- **Prayers** – A praying student is an excellent student because the "fervent prayer" of that student "availeth much" (James 5:16). Praying is the best way to communicate with God. Cultivate the habit of praying fervently with understanding while making your requests known to God.

- **Giving** – Our English teacher once assigned the senior class to give something to someone who can't repay us as we studied for our final exams in high school. For the most part, we completed that assignment. Givers can never lack because the hand of a giver is always open to receive blessings. Start giving today to people that need your help.

- **Tithing** – Although there are various viewpoints on tithing, I adhere to the Bible's position and bring my tithes to "God's storehouse so that there will be meat in his house" (Malachi 3:10). Some would claim that preachers spend these tithes, for themselves. Friend, that is not your business at all. Do what God has instructed you to do, and you will prosper.

- **Honor your parents** – A child who fails to praise their parents has automatically failed at one basic expectation from a child. Never do anything that will provoke your parents to proclaim bad words upon your life because it can be fatal. Be the child they want you to be by being gentle, humble, and meek.

- **Put God first** – When you start anything without God, it is bound to fail. In your education and your life, let God take the first position. He remains the author and the finisher of your faith, so put Him first and do not attempt to share that position with him. Let your heart be sold out completely for God. When it comes to God, any other thing becomes secondary.

If you can use these five principles judiciously, I can guarantee that you will always reach new heights because, with God, there are no roadblocks or obstacles. You're on a highway to greatness.

CONCLUSION

o · · · · · · · · o

BEGIN TO
RAISE THE BAR

"Celebrate what you have accomplished, but raise the bar a little higher each time you succeed."
– Mia Hamm

It takes a lot of work to finish a book of this caliber. You have demonstrated that you are indeed destined for greatness in life, and for that, I congratulate you. However, taking the horse to the river for a drink is one thing; the horse making the decision to drink is quite another. It has been a pleasure for me to walk you through my high school years while giving you advice and real-world lessons that will help you succeed not just in high school but in life as a whole.

The scary part is that you have such a long journey ahead of you, but when you put all that you have learned here into practice, I have no doubt in my heart that you will succeed. Everyone has the potential to be excellent, but only those who are willing to put themselves through the wringer to become excellent, do so. The fire that burns inside of you is meant to glow and light up the lives of others around you.

A glowing splint can be rekindled by placing it in a container with oxygen gas. Understand why? You cannot survive without oxygen because it sustains life. It is essential for you to fulfill your purpose in order to make a meaningful contribution to the world. Like oxygen, you have a purpose in your school and on the planet as a whole.

The things you are enjoying in the world today are because certain radical individuals decided to do something positively radical and today, we have light bulbs, telephones, airplanes, the internet, cryptocurrency, and so on. All of these men and women have left their mark on history and their legacies will live on, why? They raised the bar.

Never ever lose your identity! You are unique, special, talented, amazing, awesome, fantastic, spectacular... I could go on and on, but only you could prove to the rest of the world that you are any of those things. It's time for you to stand up, so get to it!

Nobody finishes a book like this and stays the same. You have been exposed to what will make you go from ordinary to extraordinary, so you must become a different version of yourself. I can't wait to hear about your amazing accomplishments. Day and night, I am eager to hear that you have done something that will have a lasting impact on humanity.

There is a spark in you. Don't conceal it. Instead, persist and turn it into a flame. For as many people who want to sit there, the top has been specially prepared. There are only a select few positions at the top for those who will push past obstacles and set the standard for others to follow. It will be a joy to learn that you have established a standard that no one can surpass. Raise the bar, my friend, is what it means to do.

You should conduct yourself as one who possesses exceptional qualities because you are rare, a unique breed, and dignified. Keep in mind that even if you have journeyed down the wrong path for a long period of time, it is still possible to turn around and go the other way. Everyone is entitled to a second chance as long as there is breath in their lungs.

I have a lot of faith in you. I have faith in your ability to succeed, and I know you will go on to become a household name.

My friend, start right away! Start the journey toward excellence. You will soon reach the top, so don't wait too long. Be the best so that those who follow you will have a good example to follow. Wouldn't it be nice to be able to say, "I resolved to be outstanding and today, I am grateful for how far I have come," tomorrow? I can see it. I can already imagine how amazing it will be—there will be a huge crowd of people there to celebrate you, and you'll be adorned with gold and precious gems. When they see you, everyone will marvel at your excellence.

When Colleen Patrick-Goudreau said, "When we raise the bar, people rise to meet it," he was undoubtedly referring to you, and I know in my heart that you will be the one to raise the next bar that people will meet!

ACKNOWLEDGEMENTS

o · · · · · · · · · o

I am indebted to the group of men and women who helped bring my ideas to life for the success of this book. Being able to share my thoughts with the world through this medium is because these amazing fellows have committed themselves to my success and I am thankful for being connected to them.

I am deeply grateful to my mother for her unfailing support. It could be said that she is committed to my success because she is my mother, but I would contend that it is because she is an exemplary woman, whose worth far exceeds that of diamonds or gold.

To Emma. Thank you for being the person who believed in me and helped me keep my dreams alive. Growing up, I was always aware of my wild imagination. However, I had begun to lose sight of the significance of those ambitions until I met you.

You have always been the good girl everyone wants you to be, Idara. Keep rising, my dear!

To my entire family, who has always supported me and reminded me to never settle for less than the best. Thank you for everything you've done and always will do for me.

Mr. Dele Aina and Mr. Sylvester Jenkins, you are both incredible mentors and fathers! Your wise counsel and presence in my life have always prepared me for success. You both are the reason I don't regret many decisions I have made in recent years. Your words have always motivated me to be better.

ACKNOWLEDGEMENTS

RAISING THE BAR AS A HIGH SCHOOL STUDENT

Mr. Taiwo Adenariwo, you are many things to me: a father, a mentor, a friend, and more; you always make me see life from a different perspective, and you never forget to tell me how proud you are of me. I will always cherish the time we spent together.

Tolu, you are a dear friend. Sometimes, I wonder whether you are human or an angel from heaven because you are too kind and peaceful. You speak and act with such elegance and grace. Thank you for editing the manuscript and providing feedback at the end of each chapter; it kept me writing. Thank you for being such important people in my life, Mrs. Ohunenese, and Mrs. Akinboboye. I am grateful to you for always making me feel special, for reading the manuscript of this book, and for constantly encouraging me to be the best I can be.

Mrs. Dozie, you made high school unforgettable for me. You were practically my mother in school, assuring me that everything would be fine and telling me that you knew I would be great. Those words accompany me wherever I go, and I will continue to love you.

I will not be writing today if not for you Mrs. Adeyemi, you saw the light in me from a young age and you brought it out. My editors, AndrewDaniels Creatives headed by Andrew and Pofunmi, you guys are the real MVPs. Keep raising bars!

Thank you, Juliana, Richard, and Treasure, for being the best friends anyone could ask for. The insights I gain from our discussions, as well as your support, mean everything to me.

My heavenly father, the Creator of the Universe; you accompany me whenever I walk through difficult terrain. When I think you're not with me, you're right beside me, and when I want to stop, you push me to continue. Thank you, Lord!

Finally, everyone who reads this book and applies the knowledge contained within it. You are on the right path, and I will keep rooting for you.

Thank you.

ABOUT THE AUTHOR

Charles is an author, speaker, and transformation specialist. He is a Future Africa Ambassador and he is passionate about business leadership. Through his youth outreach program, he has reached out to thousands of youths in Nigeria and across the world.

He is the host of the Youth Evolution series and a recipient of several awards and laurels. He is currently a student of Stockton University. He believes that everyone has the potential to achieve excellence and he has decided to dedicate his life to raise exceptional leaders and bar-raisers.

CONNECT WITH CHARLES

It has always been my desire to connect with exceptional individuals who are inspired to be the best in whatever they do. This desire has made me committed to sharing knowledge with people and being willing to learn from them too.

Thus, I would love to walk with you on your bar-raising journey. If you ever want to start a conversation with me about one of the concepts in this book, you can send an email to officialcharlesoc@gmail.com.

I would be glad to discuss with you.

Made in the USA
Middletown, DE
15 September 2023

38482607R00066